T E N N   A M S

A Streetca re

W
P

ME

Methuen Drama Student Edition

10 9 8 7 6 5 4

This edition first published in Great Britain in 1984
by Methuen London Ltd, by arrangement with
Secker & Warburg Ltd
Reissued with corrections 1988
Reissued with a new cover design 1994
Reissued with additional material and a new cover design 2005

Methuen Drama
A & C Black Publishers Ltd
36 Soho Square
London W1D 3QY

A CIP catalogue record for this book is available from the British Library

ISBN 978-0-413-51890-3

Set by Word & Pictures Ltd., London SE19
Printed and bound in Great Britain by
CPI Cox & Wyman, Reading, RG1 8EX

All photographs reproduced courtesy of Warner Bros.

Contents

Tennessee Williams: 1911–1983   v

Plot   xii

Commentary   xiv
    Williams's writing: repressed self-knowledge?   xiv
    An American context   xviii
    Structure: eleven one-act plays united by a purpose?   xxviii
    From *The Poker Night* to *Streetcar*: approaches to character   xxxi
    Poet of the theatre/successful showman?   xliii

Further reading   xlix

A STREETCAR NAMED DESIRE   1

Notes   91

Stills from the 1951 film version directed by Elia Kazan   114

Questions for further study   127

Tennessee Williams: 1911-1983

1911   March 26: Thomas Lanier (later Tennessee Williams) was born in
       Columbus, Mississippi. He had a younger brother and a younger
       sister, Rose, to whom he was devoted. Despite a period of
       serious illness, lasting nearly two years, his early childhood
       was happy:

> Before I was eight my life was completely unshadowed by
> fear. [...] My sister and I were gloriously happy. [...] And
> in the evenings, when the white moonlight streamed over our
> bed, before we were asleep, our Negro nurse Ozzie, as warm
> and black as a moonless Mississippi night, would lean above
> our bed, telling in a low, rich voice her amazing tales about
> foxes and bears and rabbits and wolves that behaved like
> human beings.
> (Edwina Dakin Williams and Lucy Freeman, *Remember Me
> to Tom*, Putnam's, New York, 1963, p. 19)

1919   The family moved to St. Louis, to an apartment which he later
       used as the model for the Wingfield home in *The Glass Menagerie*.
       Tom was sent to a public (state) school, where he was unhappy.

> At the age of fourteen I discovered writing as an escape from
> a world of reality in which I felt acutely uncomfortable. It
> immediately became my place of retreat, my cave, my
> refuge. From what? From being called a sissy by the
> neighbourhood kids, and 'Miss Nancy' by my father, because
> I would rather read books in my grandfather's large and
> classical library than play marbles and baseball and other
> normal kid games, a result of a severe childhood illness and
> of excessive attachment to the female members of my family,
> who had coaxed me back into life.
> (Foreword to *Sweet Bird of Youth*)

1927   April: an essay, 'Can a Good Wife be a Good Sport?', was
       published in *Smart Set*.
1928   August: a story, 'The Vengeance of Nitrocis', was accepted by
       Weird Tales.

1929   He became a student at the University of Missouri.

1931- During the Depression his father insisted that he leave university
1934   and work with the shoe company that employed his father. Tom
       kept up his writing at night, finally making himself ill. He later
       acknowledged the value of this experience: 'I learned about
       people's lives in the little white collar job class.' (Letter to
       Kenneth Tynan, 26.7.1955.)

1935   July: a farce, called *Cairo, Shanghai, Bombay*, was produced in
       Memphis, Tennessee, where Tom was convalescing.

1936   A small theatre group, the Mummers at Washington University,
       St. Louis, produced a one-act and two longer plays: *Candles in
       the Sun* and *Fugitive Kind*. He became a student at the State
       University of Iowa, now calling himself Tennessee, instead
       of Tom.

1937   During his absence a pre-frontal lobotomy was performed on his
       sister, Rose. He felt guilty about not being at home to protect
       her; his mother blamed his father for the decision:

           Right after his [Tom's] departure, my husband and I were
           faced with a drastic decision. Rose had grown more
           withdrawn and helpless, and her fantasies of being poisoned
           and murdered more intense. Cornelius decided to commit her
           to a state mental hospital. (*Remember me to Tom*, p. 84.)

1938- He spent several months moving about America, writing, staying
1940   in Chicago, St. Louis, New Orleans, California and Mexico.

1939   The judges of the Group Theatre Play Contest made a special
       award to Williams's *American Blues* (three one-act plays).

1940   An agent, Audrey Wood, managed to secure for him a Rockefeller
       fellowship worth $1000. Williams joined an advanced playwriting
       seminar at the New School, New York.
       December: *Battle of Angels* opened in Boston. It flopped. The
       Theatre Guild granted him $2000 to rewrite the play, justifying
       this in a letter to subscribers:

           We chose it because we felt the young author had genuine
           poetic gifts and an interesting insight into a particular
           American scene.

1940   Williams had a further, small grant from the Rockefeller
       Foundation, but eked it out by taking various short-term jobs,
       such as waiter, for nearly three years.

1943   After help from Audrey Wood, Williams was given a contract as a

script writer for MGM. None of his scripts was accepted. During
this time he wrote *The Glass Menagerie*.

His grandmother — a loved and powerful influence on him —
died of cancer.

1944 He won an American Academy of Arts and Letters award,
worth $1,000.

December: *The Glass Menagerie* opened in Chicago.

1945 March: *The Glass Menagerie* opened in New York, winning the
New York Drama Critics Circle Award and the $1500 Howard
Memorial Award given by the Playwrights Company.

September: *You Touched Me* had 100 performances in New York.

1946 Williams finished *27 Wagons Full of Cotton and Other Plays*.

1947 November: *A Streetcar Named Desire* opened in Boston.

December 3: *A Streetcar Named Desire* opened in New York to
enthusiastic reviews; it ran for 855 performances:

> The new play is full-scale — throbbingly alive, compassionate,
> heart-wrenchingly human. (*New York Daily News*, 4.12.1947)

> Tennessee William's new play is a feverish, squalid,
> tumultuous, painful, steadily arresting and oddly touching
> study of feminine decay along the lower Mississippi. (*New
> York Post*, 4.12.1947)

There were one or two less glowing assessments:

> His play [. . .] remains largely a theatrical shocker which,
> while it may shock the emotions of its audience, doesn't in
> the slightest shock them into any spiritual education. [. . .] It
> is, in other words, highly successful theatre and highly
> successful showmanship, but considerably less than that as
> critically secure drama. (*New York Journal — American*
> 15.12.1947)

> That the play is not merely the ugly, distressing and possibly
> unnecessary thing which any outline must suggest is due, I
> suppose, in part to its sincerity, even more to that fact that
> the whole seems to be contemplated with genuine
> compassion and not, as is the case with so much modern
> writing about the lower depths, merely with relish. (*The
> Nation*, 20.12.1947)

Williams won the New York Drama Critics Circle Award for the
second time, also a Pulitzer Prize.

His parents separated.

1948   He published *One Arm and Other Stories*.

October: *Summer and Smoke* opened in New York.

Williams visited Rome for the first time.

1949   Laurence Olivier directed *A Streetcar Named Desire* in London.

1950   July: *A Streetcar Named Desire* opened in Paris.

The film of *The Glass Menagerie* was released.

The Roman Spring of Mrs. Stone, a novel, was published.

1951   February: *The Rose Tattoo* opened in New York, and ran for 300 performances.

A Streetcar Named Desire was filmed, directed by Elia Kazan.

I Rise in Flame, Cried the Phoenix was published.

1952   Williams was elected to the National Institute of Arts and Letters.

1953   March: *Camino Real* opened in New York for 60 performances.

1955   March: *Cat on a Hot Tin Roof* opened in New York, winning Williams his third Drama Critics Circle Award and his second Pulitzer Price. It had 79 performances.

His grandfather died. *The Rose Tattoo* was filmed.

1956   Elia Kazan directed the film of Williams's *Baby Doll*.

1957   Williams undertook a course of psychoanalysis. His father died.

March: *Orpheus Descending* opened in New York. *The Fugitive Kind* was filmed.

1958   January: *Something Unspoken* and *Suddenly Last Summer* opened off-Broadway in New York, under the title *Garden District*.

1959   March: *Sweet Bird of Youth* opened in New York and ran for 95 performances.

Joseph L. Mankiewicz directed the film of *Suddenly Last Summer*.

1960   November: *Period of Adjustment* opened in New York and ran for 132 performances.

1961   December: *The Night of the Iguana* opened in New York and ran for 316 performances.

1962   The film of *Sweet Bird of Youth* was released.

1963   January: *The Milk Train Doesn't Stop Here Any More* opened in New York, for 69 performances.

1964   *The Night of the Iguana* was filmed.

1966   February: *Slapstick Tragedy* had seven performances in New York.

April: *Eccentricities of a Nightingale* was produced in Washington.

1968   March: *Seven Descents of Myrtle* had 29 performances in

New York.

1969   January: Williams became a Roman Catholic.
        May: *In the Bar of a Tokyo Hotel* opened off-Broadway for
        29 performances, winning awards from the National Institute of
        Arts and Letters and from the Academy of Arts and Letters.

1972   April: *Small Craft Warnings* opened off-Broadway and ran for
        200 performances.

1973   March: *Out Cry* had 13 performances off-Broadway.

1975   June: *The Red Devil Battery Sign* opened in Boston.
        Williams published his *Memoirs*. He was elected to a three-year
        term on the governing council of the Dramatists Guild.

1976   Williams was president of the jury at the Cannes Film Festival.

1977   May: *Vieux Carré* had 5 performances in New York.

1977- Williams contributed a number of articles and short stories to
1980   journals such as *Esquire*, *Time* and the *New Yorker*.

1983   March: Tennessee Williams died.

> He did have a nightmarish, tortured sense of the abyss and a
> smiling, compassionate complicity with those who hurtle into
> it. [. . .] The trouble with Williams was that, unlike the truest
> kind of genius, he did not grow artistically. After his best
> plays (of 1944 and 1947) came his good but uneven plays,
> after which came worse and worse ones, some still streaked
> with lightning flashes of splendour, some utterly lost in the
> murk of mechanistic iteration and self-parody. (John Simon,
> *New York*, 31.3.83)

Plot

Scene I

On an evening in early May, Blanche Dubois arrives at Elysian Fields in New Orleans to find her younger sister, Stella, with whom she hopes to stay. She is disconcerted to discover that Stella, who is married to Stanley Kowalski, the son of Polish immigrants, has a small apartment in a shabby house in the French Quarter (Vieux Carré). Blanche is evidently nervous and helps herself to a drink of whisky. When Stella returns, Blanche greets her excitedly but cannot conceal her shock at Stella's way of life. Stella, however, is happy, fulfilled by her relationship with Stanley. Blanche defensively confesses to the loss of Belle Reve, their family home in Mississippi, to pay off debts accumulated, she claims, through the dissipations and deaths of older generations of the Dubois family. Stanley returns with two friends: Steve lives upstairs with his assertive wife, Eunice; Mitch lives with his invalid mother. Stanley accepts Blanche's presence with good humour but little ceremony. She is ruffled by his lack of refinement. She reveals that she was married when very young and that her husband died.

Scene II

The following evening, while Blanche is in the bath, Stella tells Stanley about the loss of Belle Reve. She is unconcerned, but he suspects Blanche of keeping to herself the profits from the sale of the estate — profits which he believes he has a legal claim to as Stella's husband. When Blanche appears, he demands to see the documents concerning Belle Reve. Blanche is distressed when he snatches a bundle of papers, poems written by her young husband, then she hands him a box full of legal documents. He justifies his attitude on the grounds of his legal rights and his concern for the future of the baby Stella is expecting. Blanche and Stella go out for an evening together, leaving the apartment free for Stanley's poker game.

Scene III

Stanley, Steve, Mitch and Pablo are still playing when Stella and Blanche return. It is nearly 2.30 in the morning. Blanche is struck by the relative gentleness and politeness of Mitch. Stanley grows more belligerently drunk; finally he hurls a radio out of the window and then hits Stella, who is immediately shepherded upstairs by Blanche. Sobered by a cold shower, Stanley calls in anguish for Stella to come back to him. Slowly she descends the stairs. They embrace, then Stanley carries her into their flat. Blanche is appalled by Stella's reconciliation with Stanley, but is soothed by Mitch.

Scene IV
Next morning Stella tries to explain to Blanche the way her relationship with Stanley works. She accepts his sporadic violence as inseparable from the passion they share. Blanche hopes to persuade Stella to leave Stanley, planning a future for herself and her sister, to be financed by an old admirer who is now apparently a millionaire. Stanley overhears part of this, but, when he appears, Stella's fierce embrace demonstrates that her loyalties remain with him.

Scene V
Upstairs Steve and Eunice are brawling. On his return from bowling, Stanley frightens Blanche by asking her about a man called Shaw and a disreputable hotel called the Flamingo in Laurel, the town where Blanche was an English teacher. When he leaves, Blanche anxiously seeks reassurance from Stella that nothing unpleasant is known about her. She is expecting Mitch for a date and is desperate for him to provide her with a secure future. Between Stella's departure and Mitch's arrival, Blanche flirts with and kisses a young man who calls to collect subscriptions for a newspaper.

Scene VI
Blanche and Mitch return from an unsuccessful evening out. Blanche is coquettish but appears offended when he tries to kiss her. She complains of Stanley's hostility. Mitch talks about his mother. Blanche then speaks of her youthful and very short-lived marriage, which was destroyed when she discovered her young husband in bed with another man: she had later voiced her disgust, and her husband had rushed out and shot himself. Mitch puts his arms around her and kisses her.

Scene VII
It is September 15th, Blanche's birthday. Blanche is singing in the bath; Stella is decorating a cake. Stanley enters, armed with the destructive truth about Blanche's recent past: she has been promiscuous, slipping out at night to answer the calls of soldiers who were returning, drunk, to

their barracks near Belle Reve, then, after leaving Belle Reve, she has lived like a prostitute in a cheap hotel while also teaching in the local school. Finally she lost her teaching post for trying to seduce a seventeen year-old pupil and was, effectively, driven out of Laurel. Stella tries to defend her sister, talking of the unhappiness of Blanche's early life and of her short-lived marriage. She is horrified to hear that Stanley has told Mitch all he knows. Blanche emerges happily from the bathroom but is frightened as she senses that something threatening has happened.

Scene VIII

As the birthday meal ends, in an atmosphere made tense by Mitch's non-appearance, Stanley erupts into fury when Stella criticises his manners. He presents Blanche with a bus ticket back to Laurel. She rushes out to be sick. Stella turns angrily on Stanley but suddenly feels the first movements of childbirth and asks him to take her to the hospital, leaving Blanche alone.

Scene IX

Mitch arrives, unshaven and a little drunk. He is hurt and angry at having been deceived. Blanche no longer denies but tries to excuse her disreputable past as being a refuge from her grief and guilt at the death of her husband. She asks for Mitch's protection, but he clumsily tries to rape her. He retreats in confusion when she calls out 'Fire!'

Scene X

Stanley returns from the hospital, to find Blanche dressed up in a crumpled evening dress and wearing a cheap tiara. She claims to have received a cable from the oil millionaire inviting her on a Caribbean cruise. Stanley becomes aggressive when Blanche starts to lie about Mitch's attitude to her. She tries to ward off Stanley's sexual advances with a broken bottle, but he disarms her easily and carries her off to the bed to rape her.

Scene XI

Some weeks later, Stanley and his friends are again playing poker. Stella is packing Blanche's trunk while Blanche is in the bathroom. Unbeknown to Blanche, they are awaiting the arrival of a doctor and a nurse from a State-run institution for the mentally sick, to which Stella has reluctantly agreed to have her sister committed. Stella has decided that she cannot believe Blanche's account of Stanley's assault upon her; for her own sake and that of her new baby, she must reject her sister and align herself with her husband. Blanche imagines that she is going on holiday with an admirer, but is frightened by the appearance of the nurse. However, when the doctor addresses her courteously, she goes willingly with him, leaving Stella in distress, holding her baby. Stanley tries to comfort her and starts to make love to her.

Commentary

Williams's writing: repressed self-knowledge?

In the introduction to a collection of letters from Tennessee Williams, Donald Windham wrote: 'his art sprang from his repressed self-knowledge' (*Tennessee Williams's Letters to Donald Windham*, London, Rinehart and Winston, 1972, p. vi). Windham went on to infer that Williams used his plays and stories as a way of translating himself into an acceptable fiction. Tennessee Williams himself often emphasised the close connection between his writing and the circumstances of his own life; he, however, did not describe the process as being an evasion of the truth nor an attempt to glamorise his own image. In interviews and articles written in his middle years, he was able to stand back from earlier experiences and observe the foundations of his work being laid down in his childhood and adolescence. Certain elements are clearly visible in both life and art; for example, the distress and guilt he felt at the lobotomy of his sister Rose (which was carried out when he was away at college) feature in *Suddenly Last Summer* where Catharine fights to remain intact in the face of Mrs. Venable's determination to destroy her memories and her mind. In his short story *The Resemblance between a Violin Case and a Coffin* Williams describes the shock of seeing a loved sister grow into a disturbingly separate young woman:

> I saw that it was all over, put away in a box like a doll no longer cared for, the magical intimacy of our childhood together. [. . .] And it was then, about that time, that I began to find life unsatisfactory as an explanation of itself and was forced to adopt the method of the artist of not explaining but putting the blocks together in some way that seems more significant to him. Which is a rather fancy way of saying that I started writing. (See *Remember Me to Tom*, p. 79)

The relationship between the aspiring writer and his shy, emotionally vulnerable young sister is also explored in *The Glass Menagerie*. In that play, too, the spirit of Miss Edwina, Williams's mother, finds a body and voice (although she herself always denied the relationship). Williams was

a sickly child, so his early years were spent close to his mother, an
intimacy heightened by Miss Edwina's dissatisfaction with her husband.
As the daughter of a Southern preacher — a man respected in his own
community — she was never wealthy, but enjoyed a degree of social
prestige when growing up, protected from poverty, insecurity or
harshness. As the disillusionment of marriage closed in on her, so her
youth glowed more rosily in retrospect, as she herself wrote:

> Life is as unpredictable as a dream. Once I was young and gay and
> danced night after night with beau after beau, the belle of the ball.
> Then a handsome young man from a fine family came along, fell
> in love the first time he saw me and asked my hand in marriage. How
> was I to know this charming youth would turn into a man of wrath
> and that I and my children would live by his side consumed by terror.
> (*Remember Me to Tom*, p. 88)

This insistent nostalgia and puzzled, defensive self-pity echo, too,
through the words of Amanda, the mother, in the first scene of *The Glass
Menagerie*:

> AMANDA. My callers were gentlemen — all! Among my callers were
> some of the most prominent young planters of the Mississippi Delta —
> planters and sons of planters! [. . .] There were the Cutrere brothers,
> Wesley and Bates. Bates was one of my bright particular beaux! He
> got in a quarrel with that wild Wainwright boy. They shot it out on
> the floor of Moon Lake Casino. Bates was shot through the stomach.
> Died in the ambulance on his way to Memphis. [. . .] And I could
> have been Mrs J. Fitzhugh, mind you! But — I picked your *father*!

It is interesting to note the reference here to the violent death of a young
man, his life apparently blighted by passion for the Southern belle in
whose memory he still has a picturesque existence. This idea becomes
more potent in *A Streetcar Named Desire*.

The father-figure in *The Glass Menagerie* is 'a telephone man who fell
in love with long distances', as Tom remarks in the opening monologue,
yet who once had an innocent look that fooled everybody, even Amanda's
father. He is conspicuous by his absence. This was a situation familiar
to Williams as a child for his father was then out on the road, selling
shoes. When he was promoted to a desk-job as sales manager, the rest of
his family huddled together, it seems, away from his rages and his
drinking and his angry disappointment in his wife and his eldest son —
a Stanley Kowalski in middle age, with all the shared sexual passion in
his marriage spent. When in middle age himself, Tennessee Williams was

able to view his father more objectively:

> His was not a nature that would comply with the accepted social
> moulds and patterns without a restlessness that would have driven
> him mad without the release of liquor and poker and wild weekends.
> (*Remember Me to Tom*, p. 202)

In a letter written from Rome in 1955 to Kenneth Tynan, Williams saw
his relationship with his father even more distinctly as simply one
element in his own emotional development:

> I used to have a terrific crush on the female members of my family,
> mother, sister, grandmother, and hated my father, a typical pattern
> for homosexuals. I've stopped hating my father. [. . .] He was not a
> man capable of examining his behaviour toward his family, or not
> capable of changing it. [. . .] I find him a tragic figure now, not one
> that I dislike any longer. (*Letters to Donald Windham*, p. 301)

Not only do Tennessee Williams's mother, sister and father appear
recognisably in the plays, but Williams was also acutely aware of the
effect on his own nature and creativity of his inheritance and upbringing.
His capacity for deep depression, for example:

> I have plunged into one of my period neuroses, I call them 'blue-devils',
> and it is like having wild-cats under my skin. They are a Williams
> family trait I suppose. Destroyed my sister's mind and made my
> father a raging drunkard. In me they take the form of interior storms
> that show remarkably little from the outside but which create a deep
> chasm between myself and all other people, even deeper than the
> relatively ordinary ones of homosexuality and being an artist. (*Letters
> to Donald Windham*, p. 91)

Williams's homosexuality figures large in his letters and *Memoirs*,
although – perhaps not surprisingly – his mother's account of him makes
no reference to it, recalling instead Tennessee Williams's childhood
affection for a local girl called Hazel, a relationship apparently wrecked
by his father. Miss Edwina explains her son's lack of a wife:

> Tom has said to me he never intends to marry. [. . .] 'I have no idea
> of ever marrying. I couldn't bear to make some woman unhappy. I'd
> be writing and forget all about her.' (*Remember Me to Tom*, p. 240)

Williams's letters to Donald Windham sometimes conjure up an
absurd caricature of himself as affectedly promiscuous and flighty,
particularly those letters written from Key West in Florida where there

was a bohemian colony and where homosexuality, although still illegal under state law, was tolerated by the authorities so long as it did not make itself widely conspicuous or troublesome. In the 'Vieux Carré' of New Orleans, too, he found an appealingly freewheeling way of life among artists, writers and jazz musicians in bars and brothels. He is reported to have said:

> If I can be said to have a home, it is in New Orleans where I've lived on and off since 1938 and which has provided me with more material than any other part of the country. I live near the main street of the Quarter which is named Royal. Down this street, running on the same tracks, are two streetcars, one named DESIRE and the other named CEMETERY. Their indiscourageable progress up and down Royal struck me as having some symbolic bearing of a broad nature on the life in the 'Vieux Carré' — and everywhere else for that matter. (Tischler, *Tennessee Williams: Rebellious Puritan*, Citadel Press, New York, p. 62)

He was somewhat defensive about this lifestyle on occasion, understandably so in view of Miss Edwina's carefully cultivated respectability.

> As the world grows worse, it seems more necessary to grasp what pleasure you can, to be selfish and blind, except in your work, and live just as much as you have a chance to. (*Letters to Donald Windham*, p. 22)

The urge to seek refuge from unhappiness in the pursuit of pleasure, however destructive to self and others, is an aspect of Blanche Dubois's fall from grace. Her horror at the discovery of her young husband's homosexuality perhaps reflects the kind of response Williams himself had encountered or feared. On the other hand, Blanche may be a 'cover' for a male character, a homosexual, given a female mask by Williams so as to avoid having to confront his own feelings about himself — an example of that ingenious self-preservation referred to by Donald Windham. In that case, Blanche's shock at finding her boy-husband in bed with another man echoes the intense jealousy and sense of betrayal which Tennessee Williams expresses in letters at the ending of a love affair. In an assessment of Williams, written after his death, Murray Kempton stressed the importance of Williams's homosexuality to his creativity.

> We cannot appreciate Tennessee Williams without putting his homo-eroticism into full account; and that may explain why women caught him more lovingly than men. [. . .] At bottom those plays of his that

live most vividly in the mind tell us about how men must look to women — ogres to be appeased, small boys to be put up with, or, if one's luck turns for the better, strangers who will accept you and keep you safe. (*New York Book Review*, 31.3.1983)

Tennessee Williams described his writing as a cathartic or purging process, a way of coming to terms with his life:

> In my case, I think my work is good in exact ratio to the degree of emotional tension which is released into it. In a sense, writing of this kind (lyric?) is a losing game, for steadily life takes away from you, bit by bit, step by step, the quality of fresh involvement, new, startling reactions to experience; the emotional reservoir is only rarely replenished, by some such crisis as I've described to you at such length and most of the time you are just 'paying out', drawing off. (*Letters to Donald Windham*, p. 306)

A Streetcar Named Desire grew out of the turbulence of Tennessee Williams's relationships, but also out of the crisis he refers to in the letter — the months in 1946 when he endured the terror of believing that he was suffering from incurable pancreatic cancer. A morbid, shuddering preoccupation with the physical ugliness and the inevitability of death permeates the whole play.

The strong connection between the experiences and relationships of Tennessee Williams's life and the events and characters of his plays explains the intensity and vividness of his writing, but it has also been seen as a limitation, not least by Williams himself:

> Frankly there must be some limitations in me as a dramatist. I can't handle people in routine situations. I must find characters who correspond to my own tensions. If these people are excessively melodramatic [. . .] well, a play must concentrate the events of a lifetime in the short span of a three-act play. Of necessity these events must be more violent than in life. (*Tennessee Williams: Rebellious Puritan*, p. 246)

An American context

The early plays of Tennessee Williams were successful in the 1940s and 1950s perhaps because they offered violence, morality, spectacle and romance in American settings, played out by characters that often managed to be both highly individual and representative of particular aspects of American life and tradition. *Streetcar* draws upon at least three of these American traditions, which had been projected effectively for twenty years by the cinema. There was a nostalgic interest in America's past, particularly in the romance of the years before and during the Civil War. Mid-twentieth century urban Americans were intrigued and charmed by the idea of the South, by the picturesque elegance of a landed élite who flaunted their inherited wealth and their studied gentility. Morality was satisfied by the knowledge that this privileged brilliance was doomed to defeat in the Civil War and would then present an image of decorative decay. Blanche Dubois and Belle Reve belong to that tradition, crystallised for a mass audience by the highly successful film of *Gone with the Wind*, starring an English actress, Vivien Leigh, who later played Blanche in the film of *Streetcar*.

Another aspect of America's past given a wide appeal through the cinema was the folklore of the Wild West. Westerns showed home-grown heroes proving their worth in combat against savages and bandits and sticking to their friends through thick and thin — just as Stanley feels bound to protect Mitch after their time together in the army. These films also reinforced an idea of women either as child-bearers and home-makers or as whores, golden-hearted or otherwise. Stella is a home-maker and child-bearer; Blanche is neither, so might then be expected to be one of the other kind and 'no good'.

If Blanche belongs to the crumbling grandeur of the Southern plantations, Stanley is a new American, an immigrant, a man of the city. He is the one amongst his group most likely to make his mark in a world of industry and commerce, a world full of machinery like cars and locomotives. He asserts his maleness and lack of refinement; where he cannot dominate sexually he uses force. He shows, perhaps, the more acceptable face of that macho urban jungle pictured in the Hollywood gangster movies of the 1930s.

Popular entertainment, principally the cinema, offered Americans certain images of what it meant to be American. This was an idea equally important to the first or second generation immigrants from Europe as to those who thought of themselves as 'real' Americans with a pedigree reaching back to the Pilgrim Fathers or the Huguenots. Tennessee Williams's early plays dealt in familiar concepts so that even when aspects of his plots or the ideas expressed were shocking, they nonetheless were accessible to a wide audience, not only on Broadway but, later, as successful films.

Theatre, during the 1920s, 30s and 40s, changed under the impact of new techniques and forms from Europe. These influences were brought to America by touring companies, by refugees from political oppression in Europe, by the influx of avant-garde films and by Americans returning from the Continent, excited by what they had seen. In the 1920s two

important theatrical groups were formed: the semi-professional
Washington Square Players in New York, and the amateur Provincetown
Players, who were associated with the early works of the dramatist
Eugene O'Neill. The Washington Square Players developed into the
wholly professional Theatre Guild which became one of the most
influential organisations in the New York theatre world. The 1920s also
saw the birth of various political groups; for example, those brought
together in the Workers' Dramatic Council. The Federal Theatre was set
up as part of Roosevelt's New Deal to encourage playwrights to use the
theatre to celebrate or at least dramatise contemporary life. In 1931 Lee
Strasberg, with Cheryl Crawford and Harold Clurman, founded the
Group Theatre, which trained a new generation of actors and directors,
Elia Kazan, for example, who later directed *Streetcar* for stage and
screen. It also encouraged young dramatists with a serious social or
political message, men like Clifford Odets, whose play *Waiting for Lefty*
(1935) called for organised action against workers to fight against their
fall in living standards. It sought 'an alliance of the men of mind, of
vision, the artists, with the People, consciously working towards this
creative end'. (Harold Clurman, *The Fervent Years*, London 1946, p. 79).
It was the Group Theatre that gave the young Tennessee Williams
significant encouragement in 1938 by giving him a special award for his
collection of one-act plays, *American Blues*. A number of American
dramatists were experimenting with a lyrical, heightened style of dialogue
and extended speeches full of vivid imagery or highly rhythmic phrases,
sometimes approaching the intensity and musicality of verse drama. This
rhetorical style was complemented by non-naturalistic staging – as in
Thornton Wilder's *Our Town* (1938) and *The Skin of Our Teeth* (1942),
or many of Eugene O'Neill's experiments in style, of which *The Hairy
Ape* (1922) will stand as an example. Here is the opening stage
direction:

> The treatment of this scene, or of any other scene in the play, should
> by no means be naturalistic. The effect sought after is a cramped
> space in the bowels of a ship, imprisoned by white steel. The lines of
> bunks, the uprights supporting them, cross each other like the steel
> framework of a cage.

Thus Tennessee Williams's early plays were borne in on a swelling tide
of new American drama now able to take possession of major theatres
in the big cities, especially New York, and to become recognisably
distinct from the European imports, while still benefiting from the new
technology and the versatility demonstrated by European theatre. The

need for a national identity had been sharpened by America's involvement in the two World Wars, as was the need to re-appraise the values and demands of American society. According to the critic Travis Bogard, through the twenties, thirties and forties many plays were concerned:

> with an aspect of the national past that gives them a strong emotional lever against the depressing present and the failure of the American dream. [. . .] The characters cling to their dreams tenaciously. [. . .] Their dreams are never fulfilled except in the fantasies of nostalgic romances and operettas. The sterner statements insist that the thrust of American materialism has destroyed all such dreams and left man destitute in a soulless world, a wasteland. (*The Revels History of Drama in English*, Vol. VIII, pp. 62-3)

A selection of drama reviews from the *New York Times* for the years 1945 to 1947 gives an impression of what New York audiences were being offered at the point when Tennessee Williams emerged as a significant writer. In 1945, along with *The Glass Menagerie*, there was a Rodgers and Hammerstein musical about a fairground roustabout's doomed romance with a nice all-American girl in a small fishing community. This was playing across the street from another Rodgers and Hammerstein show, *Oklahoma*, a lyrical celebration of America's mid-West where farmers and cowboys learned to live and love in energetically choreographed harmony. At the same time, Elia Kazan — first director of *A Streetcar Named Desire* — was directing *Deep Are the Roots* by Arnaud D'Usseau, a play dealing with the position of negroes in the American South. Also in production was *Home of the Brave* by Arthur Laurents about the experiences of a young Jewish soldier in the Pacific campaign of World War II. During 1946 New York saw translations of Anouilh's *Antigone*, Rostand's *Cyrano de Bergerac* and Satre's *Huis Clos*. An English company led by Laurence Olivier brought over a version by W.B. Yeats of Sophocles' *Oedipus*, as well as Sheridan's *The Critic*. There was a production of Oscar Wilde's *Lady Windermere's Fan* (described by the critic Brooks Atkinson as 'a trifle seedy') and of Shakespeare's *Henry VIII*. The most conspicuously American production was another musical — this time combining showground glamour with Wild West nostalgia — *Annie Get Your Gun* by Irving Berlin.

1947, similarly, offered home-grown musicals, such as the rather fey *Brigadoon* and *Finian's Rainbow* as well as the more serious *Street Scene*, based on a play by Elmer Rice, with music by Kurt Weill. *Street Scene* was praised by Brooks Atkinson as 'a musical play of magnificence and glory [. . .] it finds the song of humanity under the argot of the New

York streets'. As in 1946, there were several imports from Europe, but there was also the successful debut of the young American writer, Arthur Miller, whose *All My Sons*, directed by Elia Kazan, dealt with the conflict for Americans between private and public loyalties in the context of the recent war. Its characters and setting were immediately identifiable by the American audience of 1947; its action was tragic. At moments the dialogue moved from the recognisably naturalistic to a more highly charged kind of rhetoric through which the questions of morality confronting the characters were imbued with a wider significance. It was enthusiastically received:

> The theatre has acquired a genuine new talent [. . .] [The play] is a pitiless analysis of character that gathers momentum all evening and concludes with both logic and dramatic impact. (Brooks Atkinson, *New York Times*, 30.1.1947)

In December 1947 came *A Streetcar Named Desire*, another Kazan production. The play was both a commercial and a critical success:

> It reveals Mr Williams as a genuinely poetic playwright whose knowledge of people is honest and thorough and whose sympathy is profoundly human. [. . .] Out of poetic imagination and ordinary compassion he has spun a poignant and luminous story. (Brooks Atkinson, *New York Times*, 4.12.1947)

Southern Roots and European Influences

Tennessee Williams was not only carried in on a twentieth-century tide of American drama dealing with the contemporary American situation, he was also buoyed up by a strong current of specifically Southern writing, which had become powerful in the nineteenth century and was still significant. Some of this literature from the South celebrated with nostalgia the chivalry and romance associated with the landowners of the Southern States prior to the Civil War (1861-65) and the doomed gallantry which became part of the folklore of the war itself. Other plays and novels, however, saw flaws in the pre-war and post-war South, while still fascinated by the South's charisma. There was, for example, William Faulkner (1897-1962), with his series of novels set in North Mississippi (thinly disguised as Yoknapatawpha County), including *The Sound and the Fury* (1929) and *Go Down Moses* (1942). Lillian Hellman in her novels *The Little Foxes* (1939) and *Another Part of the Forest* (1946) showed treachery, greed and ambition in an Alabama family, the Hubbards, using melodrama as a vehicle for morality — it was an indictment of that materialism which she felt was corroding the once bright metal of American society.

Colouring this writing was the influence – still strong in the South – of the Scottish writer Sir Walter Scott (1771-1832), whose historical romances such as *Kenilworth*, *The Talisman* and *Ivanhoe* drew upon a picturesque notion of medieval and sixteenth-century courtliness, the chivalric clash between good and evil amidst castellated towers or the pavilions of crusading knights. Nineteenth-century European Gothic fiction (supernatural melodramas in feudal locations) found an echo in the macabre tales of the American writer Edgar Allan Poe (1809-49), such as *Fall of the House of Usher* (1839), and in Nathaniel Hawthorne's *Twice-Told Tales* (1857) and *The Scarlet Letter* (1859). Both men were still much in vogue in the twentieth century with Poe in particular being seized on by the cinema as well. The quivering horror of Tennessee Williams's Blanche Dubois in the face of the city's squalid vitality and her accounts of the sickness eating away at the splendour that had once been Belle Reve recall Poe's story of the decline of the Ushers, whose painfully acute sensibility, both physical and emotional, rendered them unfit for life outside their decaying mansion in which they too decayed with a diseased beauty.

Tennessee Williams's work grew not only out of this courtly-Gothic Southern heritage, but also out of a European culture that offered writers as attractive to him yet as diverse as the Russian playwright and story-writer, Chekhov (1860-1904), the Swedish dramatist Strindberg (1849-1912), the Norwegian playwright Ibsen (1828-1906) and the English novelist D.H. Lawrence (1885-1930). Ibsen's influence on American drama can be seen also in the early plays of Arthur Miller: tragedy moved out of the courts of princes and the heroic past, into a recognisably contemporary setting, concerning itself with the middle classes or with semi-skilled workers living in the crowded city suburbs of a money-making nation. In many of Ibsen's dramas, such as *Rosmersholm* or *Ghosts*, the action shows the eruption of some guilt, thought to be safely buried in the past, into the carefully constructed respectability of middle-class family life. The dramatic tension becomes more powerful as the audience grows more aware of the degree of pretence involved in the characters' image of themselves and senses the gradual but relentless revelation of a once-submerged horror. The climax comes when the central characters suffer the confrontation of past and present: the thing they have fled from corners them. Then they either acknowledge the justness of this and endure retribution for past guilt with the dignity traditionally associated with a tragic protagonist, or they may try to retreat even further into pretence, perhaps into madness. This tragic model was well suited to Tennessee Williams for it offered a means of dramatising through vividly characterised and recognisable individuals his sense of the South's past being still active and often destructive in modern America.

> A Streetcar Named Desire makes it clear that for Williams the act of fleeing always becomes the act of reliving the past. Flight forces the presence of the past on his characters as the presence of what they attempted to flee. (Donald Pease in Tennessee Williams: A Tribute, p. 840)

A Streetcar Named Desire shows the conflict between traditional values: an old-world graciousness and beauty running decoratively to seed versus the thrusting, rough-edged, physically aggressive materialism of the new world. The presentation of a way of life is closely bound up with the evocation of a particular place; this 'place' both defines and explains those characters who are identified with it, and so the chopping down of a long-prized orchard or the gradual dissipation of an ancient estate gives expression to the decline of those characters themselves and of their sort of world. In this, Tennessee Williams harks back to images and emotions present in the plays of Anton Chekhov. Blanche Dubois is of the same breed as Chekhov's charming, elegantly selfish, admiration-seeking, ageing women, such as Madame Arkadina in The Seagull (1895) and Madame Ranevsky in The Cherry Orchard (1903). Interestingly Blanche explains that her name means 'White woods,' (p. 30), 'Like an orchard in spring!' But whereas Chekhov's women are still vivaciously staving off despair and the admission of defeat, Blanche is seen in her final struggles.

In A Streetcar Named Desire the conflict between two ways of life is concentrated within the battle between Blanche and Stanley. The old civilisation vested in Blanche is demonstrably decadent; her only means of survival in the modern world is to batten onto someone else and live off their emotional, physical and material resources, like a decorative fungus. Stanley is full of aggressive, virile energy, both contemptuous of and intrigued by the once privileged gentility of the Belle Reve world. The dramatisation of such a clash in sexual terms — the old world associated with febrile femininity, the new with a charismatic but brutal masculinity — had been tried earlier by August Strindberg. There are some interesting parallels between Streetcar and Strindberg's Miss Julie (1888). In his preface to Miss Julie Strindberg outlined his objectives and analysed the response he anticipated for his characters. He justified his choice of subject:

> It is still tragic to see one on whom fortune has smiled go under,
> much more to see a line die out. [. . .] The fact that the heroine
> arouses our sympathy is merely due to our weakness in not being able
> to resist a feeling of fear lest the same fate should befall us. [. . .] I
> have suggested many possible motivations for Miss Julie's unhappy
> fate. The passionate character of her mother; the upbringing
> misguidedly inflicted on her by her father; her own character; and the
> suggestive effect of her fiancé upon her weak and degenerate brain.

Strindberg referred to

> that innate or acquired sense of honour which the upper-classes
> inherit. [. . .] It is very beautiful, but nowadays it is fatal to the
> continuation of the species. [. . .] The servant Jean is the type who
> founds a species, we trace the process of differentiation.

Strindberg saw Jean's survival and strength as arising less from his class
origins than from his masculinity.

> Sexually he is an aristocrat by virtue of his masculine strength, his
> more finely developed senses and his ability to seize the initiative.
> His sense of inferiority arises chiefly from the social *milieu* in which
> he temporarily finds himself. (Author's Preface to *Miss Julie*:
> *Strindberg: Plays One*, translated by Michael Meyer, London,
> Methuen, 1976, p. 92-98)

Strindberg emphasises a deliberate naturalism both in the setting of the
play — the large kitchen of a Swedish manor house, on a midsummer's
eve — and in its references to the routines of life. However, both Miss
Julie and Jean can speak in heightened prose, using imagery and thought-
associations which give the play a poetic, more universal quality. In this,
too, *Streetcar* is reminiscent of *Miss Julie*:

> MISS JULIE: I have a dream which recurs from time to time, and I'm
> reminded of it now. I've climbed to the top of a pillar, am sitting there,
> and I can see no way to descend. When I look down, I become dizzy,
> but I must come down — but I haven't the courage to jump. [. . .]
> JEAN: No. I dream I'm lying under a high tree in a dark wood. I want
> to climb, up, up to the top, and look round over the bright landscape
> where the sun is shining — plunder the bird's nest up there where the
> gold eggs lie. (*Strindberg: Plays One*, translated by Michael Meyer,
> London, Methuen 1976, p. 116)

In *Streetcar* Stanley's syntax remains unrefined, but his words are nonetheless imaginative:

> STANLEY: I was common as dirt. You showed me the snapshot of
> the place with the columns. I pulled you down off them columns and
> how you loved it, having them coloured lights going! (p. 68)

Another writer who deals with the clash of lifestyles and moralities
often in sexual terms and in heightened language is D.H. Lawrence.
Tennessee Williams's early admiration for Lawrence was noticed and
lamented by his mother, who felt that Lawrence's writing lacked delicacy.

> One afternoon he walked in with a copy of *Lady Chatterley's Lover*.
> I picked it up for a look — Tom said I had a veritable genius for
> opening always to the most lurid pages of a book — and was shocked
> by the candour of the love scenes. [. . .] I didn't like the book or
> D.H. Lawrence as a person. [. . .] I didn't admire anything I heard
> about his character or how he treated his wife, who deserted her
> husband and children for him. The one play of Tom's I have not read
> or seen is *I Rise in Flame, Cried the Phoenix*, his poetic version of
> Lawrence's last few hours on earth. (*Remember Me to Tom*, p. 33)

It is in *Lady Chatterley's Lover* that Lawrence describes the meeting
rather than the conflict between a woman of the upper class and a man
of peasant stock (though educated and sensitive enough not to be a
prisoner of his class). The conflict is between that virile new man and the
effete aristocracy from which his mistress comes — much as Stanley
challenges Stella's family origins rather than Stella herself. Like Stella,
Constance Chatterley is happy to be pulled off her column and to have
the coloured lights going. After the gamekeeper, Mellors, has made love
to her,

> in her heart the queer wonder of him was awakened. A man! The
> strange potency of manhood upon her. [. . .] She crept nearer to him,
> nearer, only to be near to the sensual wonder of him. (*Lady
> Chatterley's Lover*, Penguin, p. 182)

Connie's sister Hilda, however, feels threatened and alienated by his
overt sexuality:

> He was looking at her with an odd, flickering smile, faintly sensual
> and appreciative.
> 'And men like you,' she said, 'ought to be segregated: justifying their
> own vulgarity and selfish lust.' (p. 256)

One justification that even Connie herself allows for the relationship is

Mellor's value as a stud, to revitalise the impotent aristocratic stock.
Similarly, Blanche sees Stanley as essentially animal, a stud:

> BLANCHE: He's just not the sort that goes for jasmine perfume! But
> maybe he's what we need to mix with our blood now that we've lost
> Belle Reve and have to go on without Belle Reve to protect us. (p. 23)

And later:

> BLANCHE: What such a man has to offer is animal force and he gave
> a wonderful exhibition of that! But the only way to live with such a
> man is to — go to bed with him! (p. 39)

In fathering Stella's child Stanley has completed his function in Blanche's
eyes, so now she feels that she and Stella can leave him behind with the
brutes and go forward to a life enriched by 'such things as art — as
poetry and music' (p. 41).

The conflict between innate sexuality and a consciously acquired
civilisation, present in *A Streetcar Named Desire*, is also a recurring
theme in Lawrence's work, often expressed in a very stylised prose full
of images drawn from nature or the elements, darkness and light, earth
and fire. Lawrence's kind of lyricism and this striving for the power of
myth through imagery infused with a sense of ritual are features observed
also in Tennessee Williams's work. For instance:

> In its sympathetic portrayal of our yearnings for transcendence, its
> realistic depiction of our inherent limitations, and its utter insistence
> on the necessity of imbuing with religious significance the rare and
> transient communion of man with his fellow, Williams's drama is a
> myth for our time. (Judith J. Thompson in *Tennessee Williams:
> A Tribute*, p. 684)

Such a response from a serious critic indicates the potency of these
images and allusions. There are many such examples of Williams's
reaching for 'religious significance':

> BLANCHE: And then the searchlight which had been turned on the
> world was turned off again and never for one moment since has there
> been any light that's stronger than this — kitchen — candle . . .
> MITCH. You need somebody. And I need somebody, too. Could it
> be — you and me, Blanche? [. . .]
> BLANCHE: Sometimes — there's God — so quickly! (p. 57)

One final instance of techniques which Lawrence and Williams share
concerns the use of 'symbolic' names. The opening passage of Lawrence's

autobiographical novel *Sons and Lovers* (1913) works on two levels: it describes the Nottinghamshire mining community in which the Morel family lives, but the names imbue the scene with the aura of myth or religious allegory:

> 'The Bottoms' succeeded to 'Hell Row'. Hell Row was a block of thatched, bulging cottages that stood by the brookside on Greenhill Lane. There lived the colliers who worked in the little gin-pits two fields away. [. . .] Mrs. Morel was not anxious to move into the Bottoms, which was already twelve years old and on the downward path, when she descended to it from Bestwood. (*Sons and Lovers*, Penguin, pp. 7-9.)

Tennessee Williams employs a similar device at the beginning of *Streetcar* when Blanche describes her journey to Stella's apartment (p. 5):

> BLANCHE: They told me to take a streetcar named Desire, and then transfer to one called Cemeteries and ride six blocks and get off at — Elysian Fields!
> EUNICE: That's where you are now.
> BLANCHE: At Elysian Fields?
> EUNICE: This here is Elysian Fields.

Structure: eleven one-act plays united by a purpose?

> The plot is simple. It moves from hope and frustration to destruction and despair. The characters themselves provide probability for every action. [. . .] Each scene is constructed like a one-act play, Williams's forte. (Tischler, pp. 140-143)

> Plot in the normal sense there is not too much of, for it is men and women in their moods of hope, despair, pretence, terror and uncertainty with whom he is concerned. Yet the play is purposeful. (Elinor Hughes, *The Boston Herald*, 4.11.1947)

> It has no plot, at least in the familiar usage of that word. It is almost unbearably tragic. (Brooks Atkinson, *New York Times*, 14.11.1947)

Plot 'in the familiar usage' implies a sequence of actions or events so organised as to give them a sense of logical progression from a beginning, through a middle, to an end that seems 'right'. What is the significance of the description of *A Streetcar Named Desire* as a collection of one-act plays? It suggests that each scene describes one situation or deals with one event fully enough for it to stand alone: with an exposition, a crisis and some kind of resolution. It is possible to approach any of the scenes in this way: scene one, for instance, introduces us to an environment, precipitates an action through the disruptive arrival into the Kowalski home of Blanche, and seems to offer a resolution in Stanley's acceptance of her. Or scene six: a man and a woman (in fact, Mitch and Blanche) return from an unsuccessful date. The audience is told why there is tension between them: he desires her, but is clumsy; she wishes to encourage him, but is anxious to preserve his respect for her. He reveals his vanities and insecurities, and gives an insight into the relationship with his mother which underpins his character. She reveals a tragedy in her past, giving an acceptably complete account of her marriage and widowing. The scene ends with them coming together — apparently a happy resolution. What welds these potentially self-sufficient segments into a cohesive play is not only the continuity of the characters, but a clear relationship between the scenes which does give a sense of progress towards the final solution and achieves a unity of subject, theme and action.

The fact that each scene contains enough information to make its action comprehensible means that certain elements recur throughout the play — the story of Blanche's past, for instance — but since their relationship to the immediate situation changes from scene to scene this does not appear merely repetitive. In the first scene, the outline of Blanche's marriage is quickly drawn as part of the initial exposition, and her extreme sensitivity to its memory demonstrated — with the symbolic sound of the polka merely a faint suggestion, having little obvious significance beyond nostalgia at that point. In scene two, the reference to Blanche's dead husband is part of her skirmishing with Stanley; it introduces the idea of her guilt but offers no further explanation. In scene six, her description of the boy she married and then destroyed, the account heightened by the now ominous strains of the polka, becomes part of the action, drawing Blanche and Mitch together for mutual support. In scene nine, Blanche offers the death of her young husband as the reason for her subsequent fall from grace, as a mitigating circumstance to lessen her guilt rather than a cause for the guilt itself. This time Mitch does not comfort her but condemns her, so her last hope of redemption by love and of future happiness — or, at least, future security — is destroyed. Each reference to the short-lived marriage strips away a layer of Blanche's protective pretence, until she is forced to stand exposed in the harsh glare of the unshaded light. When what she *really is* is then rejected, there is no other possibility left for her except retreat into an enclosed world of her dreams. The play's tension and energy come from the audience's growing awareness of the past rising inexorably to the surface where it will erupt explosively into the present; it is this which gives *Streetcar* its sense of being 'purposeful'.

The structure of the play departs from well-established theatrical practice in having no act divisions. The eleven scenes follow upon each other without any formalised arrangement into three, four or five phrases. This is appropriate to a sense of the relentless movement towards Blanche's final catastrophe. It is also, perhaps, a product of Tennessee Williams's experiences as a screen writer in Hollywood: writing for the cinema rather than the theatre most often requires the dramatist to think in terms of a sustained sequence of relatively short episodes, capitalising on the effects made possible by crisp cutting from one image or event to the next. It is worth noting that many of his plays have transferred to the screen with considerable success.

Although the play is also concerned with the relationship between Stella and Stanley, Blanche is the organising factor: the action begins with her arrival and ends as she is led away to the mental hospital. It is significant, however, that the action is confined within the Kowalski apartment and its immediate surroundings; we do not, for instance, travel with Blanche from Laurel or on to the state institution. By maintaining this 'unity of place' Williams is doing more than merely following the 'rules' laid down by Aristotle for classic drama. He is also drawing attention to the fact that *Streetcar* explores the continuing human need to secure a territory, a home, and defend it against intruders. This is a basic animal drive, well described by Konrad Lorenz in *On Aggression* (London, Methuen, 1966). Professor Lorenz progresses from a study of aggression and appeasement patterns in animals, linked to the demands of territorial possession, sexual effectiveness and self-preservation, to a view of human behaviour as displaying essentially the same patterns, although sometimes in a more oblique or sophisticated form. The rituals of threat, appeasement, sexual display, defence and retreat have the power to involve an audience because they appeal to deeply rooted responses which are universal and vigorous. The plot of *A Streetcar Named Desire* is, in part, Stanley's recognition of Blanche as a potentially dangerous invader of his territory; he cannot, as some animals might, accept her as part of his herd of brood mares, or, in human terms, as an addition to his harem. The impossibility of such an arrangement is demonstrated when he rapes her; Blanche is not shown accepting this as an initiation into a new role within Stanley's household, and Stella is prepared to cast her sister out rather than allow her to remain as a rival for Stanley's favours. Earlier on, Blanche makes a bid for possession of

Stella when she tries to persuade her sister to leave Stanley and set up a new home with her. In both phases of the struggle, Blanche is defeated.

It has been suggested that what might be regarded primarily as a plot decision — a basis for the selection and organisation of events — is more importantly the key to the playwright's intended 'message' and moral attitude. By setting the play in the Kowalskis' territory, Tennessee Williams is possibly indicating that Stella and Stanley are rightly the survivors in their world of vitality and birth, whereas Blanche's world is Belle Reve, a place of decayed gentility, of death, which must be rejected if life is to go on.

From *The Poker Night* to *Streetcar*: approaches to character
Tennessee Williams arrived at *A Streetcar Named Desire* through a series of stages, called variously *The Poker Night*, *The Primary Colors* and *The Moth*, gradually building up the plot and characters from a basic situation involving an unmarried teacher meeting a prospective husband while on a visit to her younger sister and brother-in-law. At first the action was set in Chicago, then Atlanta in Georgia, then in New Orleans. Originally the central family was Italian, then the brother-in-law became Irish while the sisters changed into Southern belles. Finally Williams settled on the Polish-American and Southern combination. Throughout all the phases, he had a fixed idea about the style of the setting:

> A symbolic link is forged between Stanley and the powerful modern engines of the railroad, and Williams once considered ending the play with Blanche throwing herself in front of the train in the freight-yards. (Vivienne Dickson in *Tennessee Williams: A Tribute*, p. 159)

Stanley's development is interesting. He begins, in the first draft, as

> 'a weakly good-looking young man. He has a playful tenderness and vivacity which would amount to effeminacy if he were not Italian'. (quoted by Vivienne Dickson, p. 163)

In his Irish phase, in *The Primary Colors*, the Stanley character — here called Ralph — becomes more assertive. Williams adds in associations with hunting and death — the character is a salesman of 'mortuary goods'. At this stage, too, Williams suggests both the character's latent femininity and his attraction to Blanche. She rejects him:

> I think you have a very wide streak of the feminine in your nature. You think you'll obscure it by acting with the greatest possible vulgarity. But what you sometimes really remind me of is a vicious

little fourteen year old girl that I've had in my class for two years.

If one remembers that view of Blanche as a disguised male, Stanley's initial effeminacy is significant in the light of Williams's homosexuality. Williams agreed in an interview that Blanche was in some ways a projection of his sense of himself; the relationship between Blanche and Stanley then becomes fraught with danger, with complications and social taboos underlying the surface conflict.

In his mature form, in *A Streetcar Named Desire*, Stanley has a force of character which has been interpreted as excitingly life-giving on the one hand, and brutally destructive on the other:

> The child of immigrants, he is the new, untamed pioneer, who brings to the South, Williams seems to be saying, a power more exuberant than destructive, a sort of power the South may have lost. (J.H. Adler, in *Tennessee Williams: A Tribute*, p. 41)

But:

> Stanley, in his ignorance and insensitivity, destroys both Blanche's hope and her illusion. He sees through her pose without understanding why she needs one. He thinks merely that she feels superior to him and he wishes to destroy her composure to make her recognise that she is the same as he, a sexual animal. (J.M. McGlinn in *Tennessee Williams: A Tribute*, p. 514)

Or:

> The conflict between Blanche and Stanley allegorizes the struggle between effeminate culture and masculine libido. (Robert Brustein, *America's New Cultural Hero*, 1958, p. 124)

Stanley has also been described as a twentieth-century Pan-Dionysus — that is, a modern embodiment of the ancient spirits of anarchic sexuality and the pursuit of pleasure, capable of impulsive cruelty to those who try to censor or confine them. Tennessee Williams's stage directions stress certain qualities in Stanley: his strength, his vitality, and his virility:

> *Animal joy in his being is implicit in all his movements and attitudes. Since earliest manhood the centre of his life has been pleasure with women, the giving and taking of it, not with weak indulgence, dependently, but with the power and pride of a richly feathered male bird among his hens.* (p. 13)

It would be interesting to know whether Tennessee Williams's reference to the brilliant cockerel amongst his hens contains any of the conscious irony there would be if he had in mind the old fable of Chanticleer, the subject of Chaucer's *Nun's Priest's Tale*. Chanticleer is a farmyard cock, a richly feathered male bird among his hens, whose sexuality is so rampant that it becomes absurd. For example, he longs to mate with his favourite hen, Pertelote, on their perch at night, but the beam is so narrow they would fall off. Then:

Real he was, he was namore aferd;	He was majestic, no longer afraid;
He fethered Pertelote twenty tyme,	He fondled Pertelote twenty times,
And trad as ofte, er that it was pryme.	And mated with her as often, before nine in the morning.
He looketh as it were a grym leoun	He looked like a merciless lion
An on his toos he rometh up and doun;	And roamed up and down on tiptoe;
Him deigned nat to sette his foot to ground.	Because he was too haughty to let his feet touch the ground.

The absurdity of the farmyard rooster as a sexual creature is also stressed in *A Streetcar Named Desire* by the story that Steve tells in scene three (p. 25). Tennessee Williams's decision to have Capricorn as Stanley's astronomical birth sign is similarly ambivalent: it carries pagan associations with the god-goat Pan, but the goat is also traditionally associated with low sexuality, animal lust (consider how Shakespeare's Iago uses it to denigrate Othello). Williams describes Stanley as 'the gaudy seed-bearer' and the images of his mind as 'crude' — both adjectives suggesting vulgarity and lack of refinement. On the other hand, Stanley's sexual pleasure is the 'complete and satisfying centre' of his character. Is there irony here? Does the phrase *expose* rather than simply *describe* Stanley's chief quality and indicate the limitations of his life? It is important to notice that Stanley is not wholly selfish in his sexuality; he gives as well as takes pleasure. Certainly he gives Stella enough to sustain their relationship, at least at this stage of their marriage. When he is shown as the unapologetic sexual male, Stanley often appears formidable; however, there are moments when his affectation of worldly wisdom can make him seem foolish — even to Stella:

STANLEY: I got an acquaintance that deals in this sort of merchandise. I'll have him in here to appraise it. I'm willing to bet you there's thousands of dollars invested in this stuff here!
STELLA: Don't be such an idiot, Stanley!
STANLEY: And what have we here? [. . .] A crown for an empress.

> STELLA: A rhinestone tiara she wore to a costume ball.
> STANLEY: What's rhinestone?
> STELLA: Next door to glass. (p. 18)

He is like a bull in a china shop, massively inept, in his ramsacking of
Blanche's papers (pp. 21-22), whereas she here emerges with some dignity
and humour. She succeeds in making him look 'somewhat sheepish', but
he regains status by revealing himself as the father of Stella's expected
child.

Stanley's code of morality is clear-cut and simple, ruthlessly so. He
defends his territory, his wife and his friends against invasion or
imposition:

> STANLEY: Mitch is a buddy of mine. We were in the same outfit
> together — Two-forty-first Engineers. We work in the same plant and
> now on the same bowling team. [. . .] I'd have that on my conscience
> the rest of my life if I knew all that stuff and let my best friend get
> caught. (p. 62)

There are areas of his self-esteem which he protects forcefully:

> STANLEY: I am not a Polack. People from Poland are Poles, not
> Polacks. But what I am is a one hundred per cent American, born and
> raised in the greatest country on earth and proud as hell of it, so don't
> ever call me a Polack. (p. 67)

Yet he is able to rape his wife's sister while his wife is in hospital giving
birth to his child. He justifies it to himself by seeing the event as
pre-determined, as if by mutual consent, like the inevitable and proper
mating of animals. Blanche's terrified defiance of him with a broken
bottle shatters the last fragile social taboos and, calling her 'Tiger — tiger',
Stanley responds to her gesture as part of a wild mating ritual. Even at
this moment there is a possible irony, a mockery beneath the dramatic
intensity, in the picture of Stanley, inflated with that 'animal joy in his
being', picking up Blanche's inert form and carrying it off. It offers an
image familiar to any cinema-goer who has seen Hollywood classics such
as the 1932 *King Kong* in which the massive ape with the sentimental
heart carries Fay Wray's limp body off to his lair. When Stanley says
(p. 81), 'We've had this date from the beginning', it is as if twentieth-
century conventions and moralities fade away in the face of the primeval
sexual drive of male to female.

It is, nonetheless, important to believe that Stanley *loves* Stella, not
merely with animal desire but with deep-seated feeling which sometimes

expresses itself with tenderness, sometimes with anguished need. When she retreats upstairs after he has hit her, he is racked by shuddering sobs and falls on his knees before her as she returns to him, before carrying her back into their dark apartment. After Blanche's departure at the end of the play, Stella sits sobbing on the steps, holding her new baby; Stanley leaves his card game to seek reassurance that she is still bound to him body and heart:

> STANLEY (*voluptuously, soothingly*). Now, honey. Now, love. Now, now love. (*He kneels beside her and his fingers find the opening of her blouse.*) Now, now, love. Now, love . . . (p. 89-90)

Elia Kazan's *Notebook for 'A Streetcar Named Desire'* traces his approach to the play as a director. Here he discusses Stanley's inner conflicts and dominant traits:

> He wants to knock no-one down. He only doesn't want to be taken advantage of. His code is simple and simple-minded. He is adjusted *now* . . . later, as his sexual powers die so will he; the trouble will come later, the 'problems'. [. . .] Why does he want to bring Blanche and, before her, Stella *down to his level*? . . . It's the hoodlum aristocrat. He's deeply dissatisfied, deeply hopeless, deeply cynical. [. . .] But Blanche he can't seem to do anything with. She can't come down to his level so he levels her with his sex. [. . .] Stanley is supremely indifferent to everything except his own pleasure and comfort. He is marvellously selfish, a miracle of sensuous self-centredness. (Included in *Twentieth Century Interpretations of 'A Streetcar Named Desire'*, Prentice-Hall, pp. 26-27)

Stella, according to Kazan, is driven by her determination to hold onto Stanley, so that even her sister becomes a possible enemy. In her marriage to Stanley her womanhood has flowered; she is about to move into a further stage of her life-cycle — to become a mother as well as a mate. Blanche not only appears as a rival for Stanley's favours, but tries to force Stella back into a childhood rôle, calling her 'Precious lamb!' and 'Blessed baby!' and ordering her about:

> BLANCHE: You hear me? I said stand up! (STELLA *complies reluctantly*.) You messy child, you, you've spilt something on that pretty white lace collar! (p. 9)

Blanche also tries to undermine Stella's belief in the worth and rightness of her marriage to Stanley:

> BLANCHE: I take it for granted that you still have sufficient memory
> of Belle Reve to find this place and these poker players impossible
> to live with. (p. 39)

Her challenge forces Stella to define the nature and value of her
relationship with Stanley. She stands by her love for him, which, it is
true, has its centre in 'things that happen between a man and a woman
in the dark — that sort of make everything else seem unimportant'
(p. 39-40). Blanche attempts to dismiss this as 'brutal desire', which will
drag Stella back with the animals in a primitive life without beauty. Her
failure is demonstrated as Stella turns to embrace Stanley 'fiercely and
in full view of Blanche' (p. 41) while Stanley smiles in triumph over his
wife's shoulder. Kazan suggests that Stella's commitment to her marriage
costs her dear:

> Stella is a refined girl who has found a kind of salvation or realization,
> *but at a terrific price*. She keeps her eyes closed, even stays in bed as
> much as possible so that she won't realise, won't *feel* the pain of this
> terrific price. [. . .] She's waiting for the dark where Stanley makes
> her feel *only him* and she has no reminder of the price she is paying.
> She wants no intrusion from the other world. (*Twentieth Century
> Interpretations*, p. 25)

It is possible to see Stella as the crucial battleground over which
Blanche and Stanley fight, possession of which ensures final victory. She
is then a key figure; her changing attitudes signal the movement of the
action. When she allows Blanche to lead her out of the apartment after
Stanley's drunken violence, the balance of power shifts towards Blanche.
When Stella chooses to return to Stanley, Blanche is left in defeat. At
the end of the play it is suggested that her loyalty is now to her child,
as she sits with the baby on the steps *outside* the apartment, weeping for
the sister she has allowed to be taken into a kind of captivity, and neither
responding to nor rejecting Stanley's advances. There are problems in
accepting Stanley's and Stella's marriage, as described by Blanche in
scene four. From a woman's viewpoint especially, there may be
disconcerting implications:

> How did Stella ever get over those critical hurdles — Stanley's table
> manners, Stanley's preference in dress? [. . .] Did Stanley rape Stella,
> too, just by way of a how-do-you-do? Do all women burn to be
> raped? Is this the locker room fantasy that is Williams's version of
> animal purity?
>   It is hard to know what is more unpleasant in this image: the overt

sentimentality it expresses, or the latent brutality it masks: a
fascination with the image of the helpless creature under the physical
domination of another, accepting his favours with tears of gratitude.
(Marion Magid in *Twentieth Century Interpretations*, p. 78)

The rhetoric here is extravagant; however, it raises an important issue. In
the play, it is suggested (only to be quickly denied) that during their
courtship Stanley's lack of refinement and his forcefulness were disguised
or, perhaps, made seem acceptable by his Master Sergeant's uniform.
Stella perhaps was wise to recognise in him the best available alternative
to the decadence of Belle Reve:

STELLA: The best I could do was make my own living, Blanche.
(p. 11)

This is Stella's self-justification for what might otherwise seem a betrayal
of her family and heritage; she asserts herself at the expense of all that
Belle Reve has stood for and Blanche has tried to cling to. To some, it is
Stella's selfishness rather than her submissiveness that characterises her:

Stella ignores the needs of others and eventually adopts her own
illusion. Life with Stanley — sex with Stanley — is her highest value.
Her refusal to accept Blanche's story of the rape is a commitment to
self-preservation rather than love, and thus Stella contributes to
Blanche's disintegration. (J.M. McGlinn in *Tennessee Williams: A
Tribute*, p. 514)

Her marriage gives her a purpose. Her new motherhood ensures a
continuing rôle even if Stanley's desire for her should fade. Blanche
offers her nothing except a return to childish dependence and both
emotional and material insecurity. The final image of the play, however,
suggests that Blanche's intrusion and expulsion have irrevocably changed
the nature of Stella's relationship with her husband and her chosen way
of life.

Blanche's outstanding characteristic, according to Kazan, is
desperation; her chief motivation is the urgent need to find protection:
'The tradition of the old South says it must be through another person.'
Her problem arises from this Southern tradition,

her notion of what a woman should be. [. . .] Because this image of
herself cannot be accomplished in reality, certainly not in the South
of our day and time, it is her effort and practice to *accomplish it in
fantasy*. Everything she does in *reality* too is coloured by this
necessity, this compulsion to be *special*.

Kazan reminds any actress attempting the rôle that it requires considerable emotional versatility — ranging from imperious self-assertion to fluttering helplessness, from feverish gaiety to pathetic terror. She must alternately alienate and engage the sympathy of the audience.

> The audience at the beginning should see her bad effect on Stella, want Stanley to tell her off. He does. He exposes her and then gradually, as they see how genuinely in pain, how actually desperate she is, how warm, tender and loving she can be (the Mitch story), how freighted with need she is — then they begin to go with her. They begin to realize that they are sitting in at the death of something extraordinary [. . .] and then they feel the tragedy. (*Twentieth Century Interpretations*, p. 22)

The tragic flaw that undermines her herioc and admirable qualities is, then, her need to be special, which isolates her from others. Allied to this is her refusal to accept what is innate in her — part, that is, of her *common* rather than her unique humanity — her sexuality. She denigrates it as mere 'brutal desire', thinking of it as 'a rattle-trap streetcar, that bangs through the Quarter, up one old narrow street and down another' (p. 40) while she yearns for a 'Cadillac convertible, must have been a block long' (p. 37) or 'a cruise of the Caribbean' (p. 76). She harbours dreams of a happy-ever-after ending to her story in which she as 'a woman of intelligence and breeding, can enrich a man's life — immeasurably!' (p. 78). She longs to be protected against the dangers of fading physical beauty and old age:

> BLANCHE: Physical beauty is passing. A transitory possession. But beauty of the mind and richness of the spirit and tenderness of the heart — and I have all of those things — aren't taken away, but grow! Increase with the years! How strange that I should be called a destitute woman! When I have all of these treasures locked in my heart. (*A choked sob comes from her.*) (p. 78)

Kazan sees *Streetcar* as resembling a classical tragedy, with Blanche like Medea or some doomed Greek heroine, pursued to madness by the Harpies within her own nature, with Nemesis (the spirit of retribution) dogging her heels and baying for vengeance against her for the death of her boy-husband and for her sinning. She is capable of exciting pity and terror in the audience — the responses described by Aristotle as the hallmarks of tragedy.

'Pity' implies a compassionate concern; the audience must be able to

believe in and care about the character. She must have, at least, a
dramatic reality. How is this created? She is given a past that makes sense
of her present and that makes her future fate both consistent and 'right'.
Stella refers to Blanche's upbringing and her sensitivity, in defence of
her behaviour (p. 58). She also speaks of Blanche's traumatic marriage
and widowing, 'an experience that — killed her illusions' (p. 61). Blanche
herself explains and justifies her desperate search for protection from
poverty and physical decline when she describes the squalid horror of

> All of those deaths! The long parade to the graveyard! Father,
> mother! Margaret, that dreadful way! So big with it, it couldn't be
> put in a coffin! But had to be burned like rubbish! [. . .] Which of
> them left us a fortune? Which of them left a cent of insurance even?
> Only poor Jessie — one hundred to pay for her coffin. That was all,
> Stella! And I with my pitiful salary at the school. (p. 12)

Blanche's early lessons have been bleak: gentility brought no lasting
earthly rewards; marriage brought pain and horror; material possessions
seeped away; the body swelled or shrivelled in death. As she says to
Mitch (who cannot understand her), *desire* seemed to be the opposite of
all that death, a possible antidote to the dying and the despair, so she
caught the habit, became addicted. In her final fantasies (p. 85), she
yearns for the hygienic expansiveness of the sea, for a picturesque death
without pain or disfigurement or loneliness ('my hand in the hand of
some nice-looking ship's doctor'), for a clean, bright funeral which will
be like a return to youthful romance, and the hope of eternal happiness
in heaven.

The Aristotelian 'terror' comes from the audience's recognition that
Blanche's destruction is inevitable, that she cannot free herself from the
contradictions of her own nature nor shake off the burden of guilt she
has carried ever since her husband's death. It is a tragic irony of her
situation that the only way she can attract the special attention she
craves, the protection she seems unable to survive without, is by
exploiting the sexuality she feels debases her and which ultimately
debars her from the hoped-for haven of a second marriage. She describes
her dilemma defensively, but with clarity:

> BLANCHE: I was never hard or self-sufficient enough. When people
> are soft — soft people have got to court the favour of hard ones,
> Stella. Have got to be seductive — put on soft colours, the colours of
> butterfly wings, and glow — make a little temporary magic just in
> order to pay for — one night's shelter. That's why I've been — not so
> awf'ly good lately. I've run for protection, Stella . . . protection. (p. 45)

To Mitch she admits without coquetry that her youth has suddenly
vanished, that all she wants is a peaceful hiding place that is more than
simply a grave, that she has lied: 'I don't tell the truth. I tell what *ought*
to be the truth. And if that is sinful, then let me be damned for it!'
(p. 72.). The 'if' is important; it leaves the moral issues unresolved.
Blanche's morality is that of the aesthete, the dedicated seeker after
beauty before all else. Like Oscar Wilde (the Anglo-Irish playwright
whose life and works were designed to celebrate beauty and wit rather
than more conventional moral standards), Blanche holds to the belief
that 'Lying, the telling of beautiful untrue things, is the proper aim of
Art' (Oscar Wilde, *Impressions*, 1891). For her, too, it is important
that her life should resemble a work of art, and that art, poetry and
music should be the flag she carries 'in this dark march toward whatever
it is we're approaching' (p. 41). It is fitting that she should be a teacher
of English. Not only does this make credible her often rather literary and
poetic language, but it also fits her search for magical beauty at the
expense of common-or-garden reality. It is her business 'to instil a bunch
of bobby-soxers and drug-store Romeos with reverence for Hawthorne
and Whitman and Poe' (p. 31). The images associated with Blanche
generally imply fragile beauty, transience: an orchard in spring, its
blossom bound to fall at the short season's end; a softly tinted butterfly
or a moth, driven to seek warmth and brilliance from a flame that will
sear its beauty then consume it.

As well as making sense in human terms, the character of Blanche
has been seen as embodying a number of concepts or themes: the Soul
subjected to physical existence and thus to 'the apishness and brutality
of matter' (Leonard Quirino in *Tennessee Williams: A Tribute*, p. 85); a
Jungian Great Mother Figure, a kind of white witch ('A Gallery of
Witches' N.M. Tischler); the representation 'in her frail spirit [of] the
decline and fall of a long line of decadent Southern aristocrats' (*New
York Daily News*, 4.12.1947); 'beauty shipwrecked on the rock of the
world's vulgarity' (*The New Republic*, 22.12.1947); 'the symbol of art
and beauty, this poor flimsy creature to whom truth is mortal' (Mary
McCarthy in *Twentieth Century Interpretations*, p. 99). Elia Kazan sees
her, on the one hand, as a doomed dinosaur approaching extinction, and,
on the other (with a male arrogance worthy of Stanley Kowalski), as:

> a heightened version, an artistic intensification of all women. That is
> what makes the play universal. Blanche's special relation to all women
> *is that she is at that critical point where the one thing above all else
> that she is dependent on — her attraction for men — is beginning to*

go. Blanche is like all women, dependent on a man, looking for one
to hang on to: only *more so*! (*Twentieth Century Interpretations*,
p. 24.)

Equally one might say that Blanche is 'an artistic intensification' of a
common male conception of 'all women', and her dependency on a man
is the expression of their commonly cherished hope — hence the play's
universality.

Mitch is important to the plot of *Streetcar* as he represents the
possibility — however pallid — of future happiness or security for
Blanche, that hope which makes her ultimate catastrophe all the more
poignant. He also serves to emphasise the strengths and vividness of both
Stanley and Blanche by offering the contrast of his own weakness and
insipidity. One feels that Blanche would have had to stoop to marry him,
to confine her nature within his soft-centred mediocrity. Mitch
sometimes emerges as a comic foil for Stanley; for example, his over-
scrupulous concern about the way he perspires seems funny after
Stanley's easy: 'My clothes're stickin' to me. Do you mind if I make
myself comfortable? (*He starts to remove his shirt*.)' (p. 14). When
Stanley charges after the pregnant Stella in drunken fury, Mitch's
response sounds positively spinsterish: 'This is terrible' (p. 31). The way
he is routed by Blanche's cries of 'Fire!' is absurd and makes Stanley's
subsequent domination of her seem all the more powerful.

In the early drafts of the play, the key struggle is between Blanche
and the prospective suitor, rather than between Blanche and her brother-
in-law. Subsequently the character becomes weaker, but in the final
stage of *A Streetcar Named Desire* Williams adds two important elements
to make Mitch's rejection of Blanche more credible, since one might
otherwise expect her to mould his weakness to answer her own needs.
Williams emphasises Mitch's reverence for and dependence on his invalid
mother, who will be outraged by Blanche's lifestyle. Also, before
confronting Blanche, Mitch has tried to nerve himself by drinking more
than he is accustomed to. It is difficult to be sure how sympathetic a
character he is meant to be: Stanley treats him with tolerant
superiority, yet feels a loyalty to him; his own gentleness and hesitancy
come as a relief after Stanley's blustering towards Blanche; his concern
for Stella's well-being and his courtesy towards Blanche are appealing
and believable. Yet his gentleness comes out of weakness rather than
strength: his advances to Blanche are hesitant because he is doubtful
of his power to please; his capacity for affection and tenderness has long
been absorbed by a sickly mother and a dead girl; he appears childish to

his friends (p. 28); he is embarrassed by his body functions (p. 52); he lacks the experience or the insight to see through Blanche's affected demureness, and then lacks the wisdom to recognise her worth once his first illusions have been shattered. He responds to Blanche's cry for help with injured self-esteem; then his attempt to take sexual advantage of her is a fiasco; even the words of his rejection of her are weak — he doesn't *think* he wants to marry her anymore. Williams describes him as clattering awkwardly down the steps and out of sight. His inadequacy highlights the desperation that drives Blanche to say (p. 47): 'I want his respect. [. . .] I want to *rest*! I want to breathe quietly again! Yes — I *want* Mitch . . . *very badly*! Just think! If it happens! I can leave here and not be anyone's problem . . .' (p. 47). There is a truth behind the account she gives Stanley of her final encounter with Mitch:

> BLANCHE: But some things are not forgivable. Deliberate cruelty is not forgivable. It is the one unforgivable thing in my opinion and it is one thing of which I have never, never been guilty. And so I told him, I said to him, Thank you, but it was foolish of me to think we could ever adapt ourselves to each other. Our ways of life are too different. We have to be realistic about such things. (p. 78)

Is Mitch guilty of 'deliberate cruelty' in that rejection of Blanche, either in its meaning or its manner? Or, like Blanche when feeling betrayed by her boy-husband, is he simply unable to cope with this new reality, so hits out like a child then runs away?

When he reappears in the final scene, he is evidently dogged by shame and an impotent fury. He splutters with incoherent rage against Stanley, using the language of their card-playing: 'You . . . you . . . you . . . Brag . . . brag . . . bull . . . bull' (p. 82). When he hears Blanche's voice, his arm becomes nerveless and *'his gaze is dissolved into space'* (p. 83). He ducks his head, as if to hide from her, and remains hunched over the table, sullen and ashamed, when the others stand to let her pass. He cannot bear to look at her; undignified and cowardly evasion is all that is left to him. Only when Blanche is fighting for survival against the grim nurse is he stung into movement, but he is blocked by Stanley and his wild accusation merely ridiculed:

> MITCH (*wildly*): You! You done this, all o' your God damn interfering with things you —
> STANLEY. Quit the blubber! (*He pushes him aside.*)
> MITCH: I'll kill you! (*He lunges and strikes at* STANLEY.)
> STANLEY: Hold this bone-headed cry-baby! (p. 88)

Mitch collapses, sobbing helplessly over the table. He, like Blanche, will have to find some way of trying to escape from the guilt and the sense of personal failure, or he will be finished. Perhaps he will translate the whole experience into a wistful memory to keep alongside his silver cigarette case from the strange, sweet, dead girl, with its significant inscription:

> And if God choose,
> I shall but love thee better — after death! (p. 29)

Poet of the theatre/successful showman?

In the letter to Tynan already referred to, Tennessee Williams describes his writing as 'lyric'. This implies two important characteristics: firstly, that the writing has a musical quality rather than being prosaic or naturalistic, and, secondly, that it is an expression of the writer's personal experience or, more significantly, of his thoughts and feelings about that experience. The 'truth' or 'reality' is, therefore, highly subjective and the play's success is dependent on the dramatist's ability to present his personal perspective on life so persuasively that, for the duration of the play at least, the audience can understand and sympathise with that personal vision. Williams was, by his own admission, engrossed by his own biography, using the colourful facts of his life to create the patterns of his work and, at the same time, using that process of translation from life to literature as a means of freeing himself from emotions and memories which otherwise haunted him.

In *A Streetcar Named Desire* there are recurring themes and terrors: death, for instance. His mother recalls Tennessee Williams saying:

> 'We are all desperately afraid of death, much more than we dare admit even to ourselves'. (*Remember Me to Tom*, p. 252)

This terror was but one element, according to Miss Edwina, in her son's general anxiety:

> Tom is so mild in looks and manner you would never suspect a violent feeling stirs in him. Yet violence is the way we fight fear and Tom has said he always had to contend with the 'adversary of fear' which gave him 'a certain tendency toward an atmosphere of hysteria and violence in my writing, an atmosphere that has existed in it from the beginning'. (*Remember Me to Tom*, p. 253)

A sense of the inexorable decay of beauty accelerated by the brutality of much of modern, urban life linked his fear of personal disintegration with his nostalgia for the tattered romance of the Old South — a nostalgia he could hardly escape, being Miss Edwina's son. She approvingly records this:

Another time he declared, 'I write out of love for the South. [. . .] But I can't expect Southerners to realize that my writing about them is an expression of love. It is out of regret for a South that no longer exists that I write of the forces that have destroyed it'. (*Remember Me to Tom*, p. 213)

The third theme dominant in much of his work, and certainly in *Streetcar*, is the nature and effects of human sexuality: its voracious energy, its disguises, the attempts made to control or domesticate it by self-consciously civilised sections of society, the subsequent conflicts, the relationship between love and lust, between emotional and physical needs.

Any poet of the theatre, rather than of the study, has a vocabulary beyond words — the three-dimensional images of the stage itself. The first production of *Streetcar* was designed by Jo Mielziner, a man who had come under the influence of German Expressionist stagecraft while working in Berlin. The wish to communicate the *feeling* of the play through its set was reflected in the sloping telegraph poles and lurid neon lights surrounding the ornate but crumbling facade of the pale old apartment house in Elysian Fields. Tennessee Williams's stage directions are emotionally coloured. At the opening of the play,

the sky that shows round the dim white building is a peculiarly tender blue, almost turquoise, which invests the scene with a kind of lyricism and gracefully attentuates the atmosphere of decay. (p. 3)

For scene three, *The Poker Night*, his directions are very specific, indicating the visual tradition he is drawing on:

There is a picture of Van Gogh's of a billiard-parlour at night. The kitchen now suggests that sort of lurid nocturnal brilliance, the raw colours of childhood's spectrum. (p. 24)

He stresses the relationship between the image of the set and the nature of the characters framed within it; the card players are *'as coarse and direct and powerful as the primary colours'*, with a childlike — or childish — lack of delicacy and sophistication, having no subtle shading or nuances. At the end of the play, when Blanche feels like a hunted animal finally at bay, Williams calls for her state of mind to be expressed visually in a wholly unnaturalistic but perhaps poetic — or theatrically shocking — way:

She rushes past him into the bedroom. Lurid reflections appear on the walls in odd, sinuous shapes. (p. 86)

These horrid reflections of her panic fade when she is soothed by the
doctor's courteous gesture. As she is led out, like someone blind, the
lyricism of the surrounding turquoise sky becomes grimly ironic.

This visual projection of Blanche's inner life is complemented by the
pattern of sound Williams calls for — primarily the use of music and
chanted street-cries — creating a ritualistic or dreamlike feeling. The
lyricism of the opening picture (p. 3) is given voice by the 'blue piano'
which, Williams explains, *'expresses the spirit of the life which goes on
here'*. It is eloquent of the *'infatuated fluency'* of the Old Quarter's
picturesquely self-consuming culture. Later the strains of a polka become
more and more insistent as the truth of Blanche's past moves closer and
closer to her present refuge. At first it is faint in the distance (p. 15),
then, as she speaks to Mitch of her widowing, the polka sounds more
strongly, in a minor key, shifting into a major key as Mitch moves
towards her with awkward compassion. When Blanche is discovered alone
at the beginning of scene nine, the polka is rapid and feverish. She sits
tense and hunched, no longer dressed in a near-virginal white but in a
scarlet robe:

> *The music is in her mind; she is drinking to escape it and the sense of
> disaster closing in on her and she seems to whisper the words of
> the song.* (p. 69)

It is important to remember when *reading* the play that the music in
Blanche's mind is also heard by the audience in the theatre. Tennessee
Williams uses a theatrical device to draw the audience into Blanche's
nightmare; she and they share the same experience at this moment and
so the audience may be persuaded to believe in the truth of this
vision. This may be felt as the power of poetry in the theatre, or it may
be seen as successful showmanship.

It is not only Blanche's passions and qualities that are expressed
through emotive sounds. Stanley, for example, is associated with the
powerful note of a locomotive engine — modern, brutally impressive
machine-muscle. In scene four (p. 40), his invasion of the sisters'
conspiracy is covered by the sound of an approaching train; so, too, is
his feigned withdrawal before his victorious reclamation of Stella. It is,
therefore, significant that when Blanche is telling Mitch of her marriage,
the most harrowing memory is signalled by the roar of an oncoming
locomotive:

> *She claps her hands to her ears and crouches over. The headlight of
> the locomotive glares into the room as it thunders past.* (p. 56)

Similarly, the beginning of the last phase of the movement towards
Stanley's rape of Blanche in scene ten is marked by the roar of an
approaching locomotive which forces Blanche to crouch and press her
fists to her ears while Stanley, grinning, waits between her and her
means of escape.

Stanley has his music, too. When he is full of anguished rage at
Stella's retreat upstairs, his violent gesture of hurling the telephone to
the floor is accompanied by *'dissonant brass and piano sounds'* (p. 33).
The transition from his howl of 'STELLAHHHHH!' to the intense
sensuality of their reunion is achieved by the moaning of a low-tone
clarinet. His sexual domination of Blanche in scene ten is blared out by
'the hot trumpet and drums from the Four Deuces'.

This deliberate orchestration of the play's emotional movement is
'lyricism' in its most literal sense. When the script is read, the lyric device
can be appraised intellectually as one of the several formal elements of
the play as a whole. The *idea* of it is interesting. In the theatre, however,
the power of these sounds is not intellectual but makes a direct appeal
to or an assault upon the audience's feelings.

The language of the play is shaped by two needs: character-
identification and thematic development. On a naturalistic level, the
characters are placed socially and individually by the words they use and
the structure of their sentences. Stanley's sentences are generally short,
with a simple syntax: challenging questions are followed by single-
statement answers, with key words hammered home:

> STANLEY: You know what luck is? Luck is believing you're lucky.
> Take at Salerno. I believed I was lucky. I figured that 4 out of 5
> would not come through but I would . . . and I did. I put that down
> as a rule. To hold front position in this rat-race you've got to believe
> you are lucky. (p. 82)

His vocabulary is drawn from his day-to-day interests: card-playing and
betting (p. 20), the popular culture of films and songs (p. 20), slang
(p. 88), lively but hackneyed over-statement (p. 18). Nonetheless, there
is a patterning of imagery, a kind of poetic rhetoric (that is, language
used deliberately to create a desired effect or to make a specific point —
here, this 'point' about those values and forces that Stanley embodies).
The language of games-playing has not only an obvious naturalistic
reference, but expresses a gambler's fatalism and his faith in his strength
as someone favoured by Fortune (p. 82). It is a male-oriented
philosophy: 'seven card *stud*' (p. 25), 'One-eyed *jacks* are wild' (p. 24),

'What do you two think you are? A pair of *queens*?' (p. 65). It supposes a way of life played by a set of rules which might seem arbitrary, even unfair, to an outsider and which must take into account the action of forces beyond human control, where the urge to compete and conquer is celebrated and losers may be called upon to surrender all they have. The poker games that Stanley is seen playing are aggressive, individualistic. Initially he is seen losing to Mitch, Blanche's most promising ally, but by the last scene he is winning every hand (p. 82).

> Depending as it does on the skilful manipulation of the hands that chance deals out, the card game is used by Williams througout *Streetcar* as a symbol of fate and of the skilful player's ability to make its decrees perform in his own favour at the expense of his opponent's misfortune, incompetence, and horror of the game itself. (L. Quirino in *Tennessee Williams: A Tribute*, p. 78)

Stanley also echoes or answers images used by Blanche. Her fear of bright light is in opposition to Stanley's delight in 'them coloured lights' that he 'gets going' with Stella. The effect of the imagery is emphasised by a strong gesture in the final scene when Stanley speaks dismissively of Blanche's impact on his life, then tears her paper lantern off the light:

> STANLEY: You left nothing here but spilt talcum and old empty perfume bottles — unless it's the paper lantern you want to take with you. You want the lantern? (*He crosses to dressing-table and seizes the paper lantern, tearing it off the light bulb, and extends it towards her. She cries out as if the lantern was herself . . .*) (p. 87)

Blanche's language, too, works both naturalistically and symbolically. With her, however, the symbolism is a more conscious part of the character's style. It is consistent with what the audience learns of her life and of her early character that she should move from breathless flirtation to deliberate rhetoric (p. 22) and scatter literary allusions through her conversation (Shakespeare, Hawthorne, Whitman and Poe). But the insistence of the motifs, like the strains of the polka, gains momentum and demands attention: there is the image of Desire as a streetcar banging (a word with sexual connotations) through the narrow thoroughfares of the Old Quarter, taking Blanche first to Cemeteries then, if she is lucky, to Elysian Fields — that area of the classical underworld reserved for the blessed. There is a bitter irony that she who seeks happiness so fervently should be driven out of Elysium as a sinner for whom there is no apparent redemption. Like a moth, to which Williams compares her, she is a creature of the night, shrinking from strong light yet fatally drawn to the flame of passion. The songs she sings, although recognisably of the period in which the play is set, comment figuratively on her situation and make her seem not so much an individual as part of that romantic tradition of 'captive maids' brought from 'the land of the sky blue water' (p. 16) into 'a Barnum and Bailey world, Just as phony as it can be [. . .] a honky-tonk parade' (p. 60), whose promise of happiness *could* be fulfilled only 'If you believed in me!' In the final scene she seems to belong to another recognisable tradition, that of Shakespeare's Ophelia — the delicate, loving maid driven to madness by the betrayals and brutality of the world she has been unluckily born into. Unlike Ophelia, Blanche does not sing in her final defeat, but she echoes Ophelia's pathos and poignant lyricism in her dreams of a beautiful death on the water and in the refrain-like repetition of key words ('sea', 'death') and the ironic purity of the cathedral chimes. So much so, that Laertes's heart-wrung response to his sister Ophelia's madness is, perhaps, the kind of response Tennessee Williams aspires to as Blanche is led away:

> Thoughts and affliction, passion, hell itself
> She turns to favour and to prettiness.

> (*Hamlet*, IV, vi)

Further reading

Tennessee William's own work
Most of William's best-known plays are available in paperback from
Penguin. These are the current volumes:

    *Cat on a Hot Tin Roof/The Milk Train Doesn't Stop Here Anymore/The Night
of the Iguana.*
    Sweet Bird of Youth/A Streetcar Named Desire/The Glass Menagerie.
    Period of Adjustment/Summer and Smoke/Small Craft Warnings.
    Rose Tattoo/Camino Real/Orpheus Descending.

Other significant writings:
    Memoirs, Doubleday, 1976
    The Roman Spring of Mrs Stone (Secker and Warburg, London,
    1957). A novel.
    Tennessee Williams's Letters to Donald Windham with introduction by
    Donald Windham (Holt, Rinehart and Winston, New York, 1977).

Writing about Williams and his work
Signi Falki, *Tennessee Williams* (Twayne Publishers, 1978): a useful
introduction to Williams, with helpful background information about the
literary traditions of the South.
John Gassner, *Dramatic Soundings* (Crown, New York, 1968): a collection
of essays about aspects of American theatre, with a discussion of
Williams's place in twentieth century American drama.
J.D. Hurrell, *Two Modern American Tragedies* (Charles Scribner's Sons,
New York, 1961): reviews and critiques of *Death of a Salesman* and
A Streetcar Named Desire.
N.M. Tischler, *Tennessee Williams: Rebellious Puritan* (Citadel Press,
New York, 1961): contains some readable and stimulating comments on
A Streetcar Named Desire, also on Williams's attitude to his work.
Edwina Dakin Williams and Lucy Freeman, *Remember Me to Tom*
(Putnam's, New York, 1963): an invaluable insight into one of the major
influences on Tennessee Williams – a mixture of anecdote, self-
justification and maternal pride. An interesting contrast to the idea of

the man presented in his *Memoirs* and *Letters to Donald Windham*. An easy
place to start.

Tennessee Williams: A Tribute edited by J. Tharpe (University Press of
Mississippi, 1977): a substantial collection of essays, many relating
specifically to *Streetcar*. Especially useful is Vivienne Dickson's essay,
'*A Streetcar Named Desire*: It's Development through the Manuscripts'.

Twentieth Century Interpretations of 'A Streetcar Named Desire' edited and
introduced by J.Y. Miller (Prentice-Hall, 1971): this contains some
interesting reviews of the early productions, as well as extracts from
Elia Kazan's notebook for his production in 1947.

On Stage: Selected Theatre Reviews from 'The New York Times' 1920-1970
(Arno Press, 1973): provides useful background material, as well as
reviews of Williams's plays.

The Revels History of Drama in English. Vol. VIII American Drama
(Methuen, London, 1977): clearly set out and usefully thorough
background material.

File on Tennessee Williams compiled by Catherine M. Arnott (Methuen,
London, 1985): contains checklist of plays with performance history,
excerpted reviews and a selection of the writer's own comments on
his work.

A STREETCAR NAMED DESIRE

And so it was I entered the broken world
To trace the visionary company of love, its voice
An instant in the wind [I know not whither hurled]
But not for long to hold each desperate choice.

"THE BROKEN TOWER" BY HART CRANE.

THE CHARACTERS

BLANCHE
STELLA
STANLEY
MITCH
EUNICE
STEVE
PABLO
A NEGRO WOMAN
A DOCTOR
A NURSE
A YOUNG COLLECTOR
A MEXICAN WOMAN
A TAMALE VENDOR

THE CAST

The first London production of this play was at the Aldwych Theatre on Wednesday, October 12th, 1949, with the following cast:

BLANCHE DUBOIS	*Vivien Leigh*
STELLA KOWALSKI	*Renee Asherson*
STANLEY KOWALSKI	*Bonar Colleano*
HAROLD MITCHELL [MITCH]	*Bernard Braden*
EUNICE HUBBEL	*Eileen Dale*
STEVE HUBBEL	*Lyn Evans*
PABLO GONZALES	*Theodore Bikel*
NEGRO WOMAN	*Bruce Howard*
A STRANGE MAN [DOCTOR]	*Sidney Monckton*
A STRANGE WOMAN [NURSE]	*Mona Lilian*
A YOUNG COLLECTOR	*John Forrest*
A MEXICAN WOMAN	*Eileen Way*

Directed by LAURENCE OLIVIER
Setting and lighting by JO MIELZINER
Costumes by BEATRICE DAWSON

SCENE I

The exterior of a two-storey corner building on a street in New Orleans which is named Elysian Fields and runs between the L & N tracks and the river. The section is poor but, unlike corresponding sections in other American cities, it has a raffish charm. The houses are mostly white frame, weathered grey, with rickety outside stairs and galleries and quaintly ornamented gables to the entrances of both. It is first dark of an evening early in May. The sky that shows around the dim white building is a peculiarly tender blue, almost turquoise, which invests the scene with a kind of lyricism and gracefully attenuates the atmosphere of decay. You can almost feel the warm breath of the brown river beyond the river warehouses with their faint redolences of bananas and coffee. A corresponding air is evoked by the music of Negro entertainers at a bar-room around the corner. In this part of New Orleans you are practically always just around the corner, or a few doors down the street, from a tinny piano being played with the infatuated fluency of brown fingers. This "Blue Piano" expresses the spirit of the life which goes on here.

> *Two women, one white and one coloured, are taking the air on the steps of the building. The white woman is* EUNICE, *who occupies the upstairs flat; the coloured woman a neighbour, for New Orleans is a cosmopolitan city where there is a relatively warm and easy intermingling of races in the old part of town.*
> *Above the music of the "Blue Piano" the voices of people on the street can be heard overlapping.*

NEGRO WOMAN [*to* EUNICE]: . . . she says St. Barnabas would send out his dog to lick her and when he did she'd feel an icy cold wave all up an' down her. Well, that night when——

A MAN [*to a* SAILOR]: You keep right on going and you'll find it. You'll hear them tapping on the shutters.

SAILOR [*to* NEGRO WOMAN *and* EUNICE]: Where's the Four Deuces?

VENDOR: Red hot! Red hots!

NEGRO WOMAN: Don't waste your money in that clip joint!

SAILOR: I've got a date there.

VENDOR: Re-e-ed h-o-o-t!

NEGRO WOMAN: Don't let them sell you a Blue Moon cocktail or you won't go out on your own feet!

Two men come around the corner, STANLEY KOWALSKI *and* MITCH. *They are about twenty-eight or thirty years old, roughly dressed in blue denim work clothes.* STANLEY *carries his bowling jacket and a red-stained package from a butcher's.]*

STANLEY [*to* MITCH]: Well, what did he say?

MITCH: He said he'd give us even money.

STANLEY: Naw! We gotta have odds!

They stop at the foot of the steps.

STANLEY [*bellowing*]: Hey, there! Stella, Baby!

STELLA *comes out on the first-floor landing, a gentle young woman, about twenty-five, and of a background obviously quite different from her husband's.*

STELLA [*mildly*]: Don't holler at me like that. Hi, Mitch.

STANLEY: Catch!

STELLA: What?

STANLEY: Meat!

He heaves the package at her. She cries out in protest but manages to catch it: then she laughs breathlessly. Her husband and his companion have already started back around the corner.

STELLA [*calling after him*]: Stanley! Where are you going?

STANLEY: Bowling!

STELLA: Can I come watch?

STANLEY: Come on. [*He goes out.*]

STELLA: Be over soon. [*To the white woman.*] Hello, Eunice. How are you?

EUNICE: I'm all right. Tell Steve to get him a poor boy's sandwich 'cause nothing's left here.

They all laugh; the COLOURED WOMAN *does not stop.* STELLA *goes out.*

COLOURED WOMAN: What was that package he th'ew at 'er? [*She rises from steps, laughing louder.*]

EUNICE: You hush, now!

NEGRO WOMAN: Catch *what*!

She continues to laugh. BLANCHE *comes around the corner, carrying a valise. She looks at a slip of paper, then at the building, then again at the slip and again at the building. Her expression is one of shocked disbelief. Her appearance is incongruous to this setting. She is daintily dressed in a white suit with a fluffy bodice, necklace and earrings of pearl, white gloves and hat, looking as if she were arriving at a summer tea or cocktail party in the garden district. She is about five years older than STELLA. Her delicate beauty must avoid a strong light. There is something about her uncertain manner, as well as her white clothes, that suggests a moth.*

EUNICE [*finally*]: What's the matter, honey? Are you lost?

BLANCHE [*with faintly hysterical humour*]: They told me to take a street-car named Desire, and then transfer to one called Cemeteries and ride six blocks and get off at—Elysian Fields!

EUNICE: That's where you are now.

BLANCHE: At Elysian Fields?

EUNICE: This here is Elysian Fields.

BLANCHE: They mustn't have—understood—what number I wanted . . .

EUNICE: What number you lookin' for?

BLANCHE *wearily refers to the slip of paper.*

BLANCHE: Six thirty-two

EUNICE: You don't have to look no further.

BLANCHE [*uncomprehendingly*]: I'm looking for my sister, Stella DuBois. I mean—Mrs. Stanley Kowalski.

EUNICE: That's the party.—You just did miss her, though.

BLANCHE: This—can this be—her home?

EUNICE: She's got the downstairs here and I got the up.

BLANCHE: Oh. She's—out?

EUNICE: You noticed that bowling alley around the corner?

BLANCHE: I'm—not sure I did.

EUNICE: Well, that's where she's at, watchin' her husband bowl. [*There is a pause.*] You want to leave your suitcase here an' go find her?

BLANCHE: No.

NEGRO WOMAN: I'll go tell her you come.

BLANCHE: Thanks.

NEGRO WOMAN: You welcome. [*She goes out.*]

EUNICE: She wasn't expecting you?

BLANCHE: No. No, not tonight.

EUNICE: Well, why don't you just go in and make yourself at home till they get back.

BLANCHE: How could I—do that?
EUNICE: We own this place so I can let you in.

She gets up and opens the downstairs door. A light goes on behind the blind, turning it light blue. BLANCHE slowly follows her into the downstairs flat. The surrounding areas dim out as the interior is lighted. Two rooms can be seen, not too clearly defined. The one first entered is primarily a kitchen but contains a folding bed to be used by BLANCHE. The room beyond this is a bedroom. Off this room is a narrow door to a bathroom.

EUNICE [*defensively, noticing* BLANCHE's *look*]: It's sort of messed up right now but when it's clean it's real sweet.
BLANCHE: Is it?
EUNICE: Uh-huh, I think so. So you're Stella's sister?
BLANCHE: Yes. [*Wanting to get rid of her.*] Thanks for letting me in.
EUNICE: *Por nada*, as the Mexicans say, *por nada*! Stella spoke of you.
BLANCHE: Yes?
EUNICE: I think she said you taught school.
BLANCHE: Yes.
EUNICE: And you're from Mississippi, huh?
BLANCHE: Yes.
EUNICE: She showed me a picture of your home-place, the plantation.
BLANCHE: Belle Reve?
EUNICE: A great big place with white columns.
BLANCHE: Yes ...
EUNICE: A place like that must be awful hard to keep up.
BLANCHE: If you will excuse me, I'm just about to drop.
EUNICE: Sure, honey. Why don't you set down?
BLANCHE: What I meant was I'd like to be left alone.
EUNICE [*offended*]: Aw. I'll make myself scarce, in that case.
BLANCHE: I didn't mean to be rude, but——
EUNICE: I'll drop by the bowling alley an' hustle her up. [*She goes out of the door.*

BLANCHE sits in a chair very stiffly with her shoulders slightly hunched and her legs pressed close together and her hands tightly clutching her purse as if she were quite cold. After a while the blind look goes out of her eyes and she begins to look slowly around. A cat screeches. She catches her breath with a startled gesture. Suddenly she notices something in a half opened closet. She springs up and crosses to it, and removes a whisky bottle. She pours a half tumbler of whisky and tosses it down. She carefully replaces the bottle and washes out the tumbler at the sink. Then she resumes her seat in front of the table.

BLANCHE [*faintly to herself*]: I've got to keep hold of myself!

STELLA comes quickly around the corner of the building and runs to the door of the downstairs flat.

STELLA [*calling out joyfully*]: Blanche!

For a moment they stare at each other. Then BLANCHE springs up and runs to her with a wild cry.

BLANCHE: Stella, oh, Stella, Stella! Stella for Star!

She begins to speak with feverish vivacity as if she feared for either of them to stop and think. They catch each other in a spasmodic embrace.

BLANCHE: Now, then, let me look at you. But don't you look at me, Stella, no, no, no, not till later, not till I've bathed and rested! And turn that over-light off! Turn that off! I won't be looked at in this merciless glare! [STELLA *laughs and complies.*] Come back here now! Oh, my baby! Stella! Stella for Star! [*She embraces her again.*] I thought you would never come back to this horrible place! What am I saying? I didn't mean to say that. I meant to be nice about it and say—Oh, what a convenient location and such—Ha-a-ha! Precious lamb! You haven't said a *word* to me.

STELLA: You haven't given me a chance to, honey! [*She laughs but her glance at* BLANCHE *is a little anxious.*]

BLANCHE: Well, now you talk. Open your pretty mouth and talk while I look around for some liquor! I know you must have some liquor on the place! Where could it be, I wonder? Oh, I spy, I spy!

She rushes to the closet and removes the bottle; she is shaking all over and panting for breath as she tries to laugh. The bottle nearly slips from her grasp.

STELLA [*noticing*]: Blanche, you sit down and let me pour the drinks. I don't know what we've got to mix with. Maybe a coke's in the icebox. Look'n see, honey, while I'm——

BLANCHE: No coke, honey, not with my nerves tonight! Where— where—where is——?

STELLA: Stanley? Bowling! He loves it. They're having a—found some soda!—tournament . . .

BLANCHE: Just water, baby, to chase it! Now don't get worried, your sister hasn't turned into a drunkard, she's just all shaken up and hot and tired and dirty! You sit down, now, and explain this place to me! What are you doing in a place like this?

STELLA: Now, Blanche——

BLANCHE: Oh, I'm not going to be hypocritical, I'm going to be honestly critical about it! Never, never, never in my worst dreams could I picture—— Only Poe! Only Mr. Edgar Allan Poe!—could do it justice! Out there I suppose is the ghoul-haunted woodland of Weir! [*She laughs.*]

STELLA: No, honey, those are the L & N tracks.

BLANCHE: No, now seriously, putting joking aside. Why didn't you tell me, why didn't you write me, honey, why didn't you let me know?

STELLA [*carefully, pouring herself a drink*]: Tell you what, Blanche?

BLANCHE: Why, that you had to live in these conditions!

STELLA: Aren't you being a little intense about it? It's not that bad at all! New Orleans isn't like other cities.

BLANCHE: This has got nothing to do with New Orleans. You might as well say—forgive me, blessed baby! [*She suddenly stops short.*] The subject is closed!

STELLA [*a little drily*]: Thanks.

   During the pause, BLANCHE *stares at her. She smiles at* BLANCHE.

BLANCHE [*looking down at her glass, which shakes in her hand*]: You're all I've got in the world, and you're not glad to see me!

STELLA [*sincerely*]: Why, Blanche, you know that's not true.

BLANCHE: No?—I'd forgotten how quiet you were.

STELLA: You never did give me a chance to say much, Blanche. So I just got in the habit of being quiet around you.

BLANCHE [*vaguely*]: A good habit to get into . . . [*then abruptly*] You haven't asked me how I happened to get away from the school before the spring term ended.

STELLA: Well, I thought you'd volunteer that information—if you wanted to tell me.

BLANCHE: You thought I'd been fired?

STELLA: No, I—thought you might have—resigned. . . .

BLANCHE: I was so exhausted by all I'd been through my—nerves broke. [*Nervously tamping cigarette.*] I was on the verge of—lunacy, almost! So Mr. Graves—Mr. Graves is the high school superinten-dent—he suggested I take a leave of absence. I couldn't put all of those details into the wire. . . . [*She drinks quickly.*] Oh, this buzzes right through me and feels so *good*!

STELLA: Won't you have another?

BLANCHE: No, one's my limit.

STELLA: Sure?

BLANCHE: You haven't said a word about my appearance.

STELLA: You look just fine.

BLANCHE: God love you for a liar! Daylight never exposed so total a ruin! But you—you've put on some weight, yes, you're just as plump as a little partridge! And it's so becoming to you!

STELLA: Now, Blanche——

BLANCHE: Yes, it is, it is or I wouldn't say it! You just have to watch around the hips a little. Stand up.

STELLA: Not now.

BLANCHE: You hear me? I said stand up! [STELLA *complies reluctantly.*] You messy child, you, you've spilt something on that pretty white lace collar! About your hair—you ought to have it cut in a feather bob with your dainty features. Stella, you have a maid, don't you?

STELLA: No. With only two rooms it's——

BLANCHE: What? *Two* rooms, did you say?

STELLA: This one and—— [*She is embarrassed.*]

BLANCHE: The other one? [*She laughs sharply. There is an embarrassed silence.*] How quiet you are, you're so peaceful. Look how you sit there with your little hands folded like a cherub in choir!

STELLA [*uncomfortably*]: I never had anything like your energy, Blanche.

BLANCHE: Well, I never had your beautiful self-control. I am going to take just one little tiny nip more, sort of to put the stopper on, so to speak. . . . Then put the bottle away so I won't be tempted. [*She rises.*] I want you to look at *my* figure! [*She turns around.*] You know I haven't put on one ounce in ten years, Stella? I weigh what I weighed the summer you left Belle Reve. The summer Dad died and you left us . . .

STELLA [*a little wearily*]: It's just incredible, Blanche, how well you're looking.

BLANCHE: You see I still have that awful vanity about my looks even now that my looks are slipping! [*She laughs nervously and glances at* STELLA *for reassurance.*]

STELLA [*dutifully*]: They haven't slipped one particle.

BLANCHE: After all I've been through? You think I believe that

story? Blessed child! [*She touches her forehead shakily.*] Stella, there's
—only two rooms?

STELLA: And a bathroom.

BLANCHE: Oh, you do have a bathroom! First door to the right at
the top of the stairs? [*They both laugh uncomfortably.*] But, Stella,
I don't see where you're going to put me!

STELLA: We're going to put you in here.

BLANCHE: What kind of bed's this—one of those collapsible things?
[*She sits on it.*]

STELLA: Does it feel all right?

BLANCHE [*dubiously*]: Wonderful, honey. I don't like a bed that
gives much. But there's no door between the two rooms, and
Stanley—will it be decent?

STELLA: Stanley is Polish, you know.

BLANCHE: Oh, yes. They're something like Irish, aren't they?

STELLA: Well——

BLANCHE: Only not so—highbrow? [*They both laugh again in the
same way.*] I brought some nice clothes to meet all your lovely
friends in.

STELLA: I'm afraid you won't think they are lovely.

BLANCHE: What are they like?

STELLA: They're Stanley's friends.

BLANCHE: Polacks?

STELLA: They're a mixed lot, Blanche.

BLANCHE: Heterogeneous—types?

STELLA: Oh, yes. Yes, types is right!

BLANCHE: Well—anyhow—I brought nice clothes and I'll wear
them. I guess you're hoping I'll say I'll put up at a hotel, but I'm
not going to put up at a hotel. I want to be *near* you, got to be *with*
somebody, I *can't* be alone! Because—as you must have noticed—
I'm—*not very well*. . . . [*Her voice drops and her look is frightened.*]

STELLA: You seem a little bit nervous or overwrought or something.

BLANCHE: Will Stanley like me, or will I be just a visiting in-law,
Stella? I couldn't stand that.

STELLA: You'll get along fine together, if you'll just try not to—
well—compare him with men that we went out with at home.

BLANCHE: Is he so—different?

STELLA: Yes. A different species.

BLANCHE: In what way; what's he like?

STELLA: Oh, you can't describe someone you're in love with!
Here's a picture of him! [*She hands a photograph to* BLANCHE.]

BLANCHE: An officer?

STELLA: A Master Sergeant in the Engineers' Corps. Those are decorations!

BLANCHE: He had those on when you met him?

STELLA: I assure you I wasn't just blinded by all the brass.

BLANCHE: That's not what I——

STELLA: But of course there were things to adjust myself to later on.

BLANCHE: Such as his civilian background! [STELLA *laughs uncertainly*.] How did he take it when you said I was coming?

STELLA: Oh, Stanley doesn't know yet.

BLANCHE [*frightened*]: You—haven't told him?

STELLA: He's on the road a good deal.

BLANCHE: Oh. Travels?

STELLA: Yes.

BLANCHE: Good. I mean—isn't it?

STELLA [*half to herself*]: I can hardly stand it when he is away for a night. . . .

BLANCHE: Why, Stella?

STELLA: When he's away for a week I nearly go wild!

BLANCE: Gracious!

STELLA: And when he comes back I cry on his lap like a baby. . . . [*She smiles to herself.*]

BLANCHE: I guess that is what is meant by being in love. . . . [STELLA *looks up with a radiant smile.*] Stella——

STELLA: What?

BLANCHE [*in an uneasy rush*]: I haven't asked you the things you probably thought I was going to ask. And so I'll expect you to be understanding about what *I* have to tell *you*.

STELLA: What, Blanche? [*Her face turns anxious.*]

BLANCHE: Well, Stella—you're going to reproach me, I know that you're bound to reproach me—but before you do—take into consideration—you left! I stayed and struggled! You came to New Orleans and looked out for yourself! *I* stayed at *Belle Reve* and tried to hold it together! I'm not meaning this in any reproachful way, but *all* the burden descended on *my* shoulders.

STELLA: The best I could do was make my own living, Blanche.

BLANCHE *begins to shake again with intensity.*

BLANCHE: I know, I know. But you are the one that abandoned Belle Reve, not I! I stayed and fought for it, bled for it, almost died for it!

STELLA: Stop this hysterical outburst and tell me what's happened? What do you mean fought and bled? What kind of——

BLANCHE: I knew you would, Stella. I knew you would take this attitude about it!

STELLA: About—what?—please!

BLANCHE [*slowly*]: The loss—the loss . . .

STELLA: Belle Reve? Lost, is it? No!

BLANCHE: Yes, Stella.

They stare at each other across the yellow-checked linoleum of the table. BLANCHE *slowly nods her head and* STELLA *looks slowly down at her hands folded on the table. The music of the "blue piano" grows louder.* BLANCHE *touches her handkerchief to her forehead.*

STELLA: But how did it go? What happened?

BLANCHE [*springing up*]: You're a fine one to ask me how it went!

STELLA: Blanche!

BLANCHE: You're a fine one to sit there *accusing me* of it!

STELLA: *Blanche!*

BLANCHE: I, I, *I* took the blows in my face and my body! All of those deaths! The long parade to the graveyard! Father, mother! Margaret, that dreadful way! So big with it, it couldn't be put in a coffin! But had to be burned like rubbish! You just came home in time for the funerals, Stella. And funerals are pretty compared to deaths. Funerals are quiet, but deaths—not always. Sometimes their breathing is hoarse, and sometimes it rattles, and sometimes they even cry out to you, "Don't let me go!" Even the old, sometimes, say, "Don't let me go." As if you were able to stop them! But funerals are quiet, with pretty flowers. And, oh, what gorgeous boxes they pack them away in! Unless you were there at the bed when they cried out, "Hold me!" you'd never suspect there was the struggle for breath and bleeding. You didn't dream, but I saw! *Saw! Saw!* And now you sit there telling me with your eyes that I let the place go! How in hell do you think all that sickness and dying was paid for? Death is expensive, Miss Stella! And old Cousin Jessie's right after Margaret's, hers! Why, the Grim Reaper had put up his tent on our doorstep! . . . Stella. Belle Reve was his headquarters! Honey—that's how it slipped through my fingers! Which of them left us a fortune? Which of them left a cent of insurance even? Only poor Jessie—one hundred to pay for her coffin. That was all, Stella! And I with my pitiful salary at the school. Yes, accuse me! Sit there and stare at me, thinking I let the place go!

I let the place go? Where were *you*. In bed with your—Polack!

STELLA [*springing*]: Blanche! You be still! That's enough! [*She starts out.*]

BLANCHE: Where are you going?

STELLA: I'm going into the bathroom to wash my face.

BLANCHE: Oh, Stella, Stella, you're crying!

STELLA: Does that surprise you?

> STELLA *goes into the bathroom.*
> *Outside is the sound of men's voices.* STANLEY, STEVE *and* MITCH *cross to the foot of the steps.*

STEVE: And the old lady is on her way to Mass and she's late and there's a cop standin' in front of th' church an' she comes runnin' up an' says, "Officer—is Mass out yet?" He looks her over and says, "No, Lady, but y'r hat's on crooked!" [*They give a hoarse bellow of laughter.*]

STEVE: Playing poker tomorrow night?

STANLEY: Yeah—at Mitch's.

MITCH: Not at my place. My mother's still sick. [*He starts off.*]

STANLEY [*calling after him*]: All right, we'll play at my place . . . but you bring the beer.

EUNICE [*hollering down from above*]: Break it up down there! I made the spaghetti dish and ate it myself.

STEVE [*going upstairs*]: I told you and phoned you we was playing. [*To the men*] Jax beer!

EUNICE: You never phoned me once.

STEVE: I told you at breakfast—and phoned you at lunch . . .

EUNICE: Well, never mind about that. You just get yourself home here once in a while.

STEVE: You want it in the papers?

> *More laughter and shouts of parting come from the men.* STANLEY *throws the screen door of the kitchen open and comes in. He is of medium height, about five feet eight or nine, and strongly, compactly built. Animal joy in his being is implicit in all his movements and attitudes. Since earliest manhood the centre of his life has been pleasure with women, the giving and taking of it, not with weak indulgence, dependently, but with the power and pride of a richly feathered male bird among hens. Branching out from this complete and satisfying centre are all the auxiliary channels of his life, such as his heartiness with men, his appreciation of rough humour, his love of good drink and food and*

games, his car, his radio, everything that is his, that bears his emblem of the gaudy seed-bearer. He sizes women up at a glance, with sexual classifications, crude images flashing into his mind and determining the way he smiles at them.

BLANCHE [*drawing involuntarily back from his stare*]: You must be Stanley. I'm Blanche.

STANLEY: Stella's sister?

BLANCHE: Yes.

STANLEY: H'lo. Where's the little woman?

BLANCHE: In the bathroom.

STANLEY: Oh. Didn't know you were coming in town.

BLANCHE: I—uh——

STANLEY: Where you from, Blanche?

BLANCHE: Why, I—live in Laurel.

He has crossed to the closet and removed the whisky bottle.

STANLEY: In Laurel, huh? Oh, yeah. Yeah, in Laurel, that's right. Not in my territory. Liquor goes fast in hot weather. [*He holds the bottle to the light to observe its depletion.*] Have a shot?

BLANCHE: No, I—rarely touch it.

STANLEY: Some people rarely touch it, but it touches them often.

BLANCHE [*faintly*]: Ha-ha.

STANLEY: My clothes're stickin' to me. Do you mind if I make myself comfortable? [*He starts to remove his shirt.*]

BLANCHE: Please, please do.

STANLEY: Be comfortable is my motto.

BLANCHE: It's mine, too. It's hard to stay looking fresh. I haven't washed or even powdered my face and—here you are!

STANLEY: You know you can catch cold sitting around in damp things, especially when you been exercising hard like bowling is. You're a teacher, aren't you?

BLANCHE: Yes.

STANLEY: What do you teach, Blanche?

BLANCHE: English.

STANLEY: I never was a very good English student. How long you here for, Blanche?

BLANCHE: I—don't know yet.

STANLEY: You going to shack up here?

BLANCHE: I thought I would if it's not inconvenient for you all.

STANLEY: Good.

BLANCHE: Travelling wears me out.

STANLEY: Well, take it easy.

A cat screeches near the window. BLANCHE *springs up.*

BLANCHE: What's that?
STANLEY: Cats. . . . Hey, Stella!
STELLA [*faintly, from the bathroom*]: Yes, Stanley.
STANLEY: Haven't fallen in, have you? [*He grins at* BLANCHE. *She tries unsuccessfully to smile back. There is a silence.*] I'm afraid I'll strike you as being the unrefined type. Stella's spoke of you a good deal. You were married once, weren't you?

The music of the polka rises up, faint in the distance.

BLANCHE: Yes. When I was quite young.
STANLEY: What happened?
BLANCHE: The boy—the boy died. [*She sinks back down.*] I'm afraid I'm—going to be sick!

Her head falls on her arms.

SCENE II

It is six o'clock the following evening. BLANCHE *is bathing.* STELLA *is completing her toilette.* BLANCHE'S *dress, a flowered print, is laid out on* STELLA'S *bed.*

> STANLEY *enters the kitchen from outside, leaving the door open on the perpetual "blue piano" around the corner.*

STANLEY: What's all this monkey doings?
STELLA: Oh, Stan! [*She jumps up and kisses him which he accepts with lordly composure.*] I'm taking Blanche to Galatoires' for supper and then to a show, because it's your poker night.
STANLEY: How about my supper, huh? I'm not going to no Galatoire's for supper!
STELLA: I put you a cold plate on ice.
STANLEY: Well, isn't that just dandy!
STELLA: I'm going to try to keep Blanche out till the party breaks up because I don't know how she would take it. So we'll go to one of the little places in the Quarter afterwards and you'd better give me some money.

STANLEY: Where is she?

STELLA: She's soaking in a hot tub to quiet her nerves. She's terribly upset.

STANLEY: Over what?

STELLA: She's been through such an ordeal.

STANLEY: Yeah?

STELLA: Stan, we've—lost Belle Reve!

STANLEY: The place in the country?

STELLA: Yes.

STANLEY: How?

STELLA [*vaguely*]: Oh, it had to be—sacrificed or something. [*There is a pause while* STANLEY *considers.* STELLA *is changing into her dress.*] When she comes in be sure to say something nice about her appearance. And, oh! Don't mention the baby. I haven't said anything yet, I'm waiting until she gets in a quieter condition.

STANLEY [*ominously*]: So?

STELLA: And try to understand her and be nice to her, Stan.

BLANCHE [*singing in the bathroom*]:

> "From the land of the sky blue water,
> They brought a captive maid!"

STELLA: She wasn't expecting to find us in such a small place. You see I'd tried to gloss things over a little in my letters.

STANLEY: So?

STELLA: And admire her dress and tell her she's looking wonderful. That's important with Blanche. Her little weakness!

STANLEY: Yeah. I get the idea. Now let's skip back a little to where you said the country place was disposed of.

STELLA: Oh!—yes . . .

STANLEY: How about that? Let's have a few more details on that subject.

STELLA: It's best not to talk much about it until she's calmed down.

STANLEY: So that's the deal, huh? Sister Blanche cannot be annoyed with business details right now!

STELLA: You saw how she was last night.

STANLEY: Uh-hum, I saw how she was. Now let's have a gander at the bill of sale.

STELLA: I haven't seen any.

STANLEY: She didn't show you no papers, no deed of sale or nothing like that, huh?

STELLA: It seems like it wasn't sold.

STANLEY: Well, what in hell was it then, give away? To charity?

STELLA: Shhh! She'll hear you.

STANLEY: I don't care if she hears me. Let's see the papers!

STELLA: There weren't any papers, she didn't show any papers, I don't care about papers.

STANLEY: Have you ever heard of the Napoleonic code?

STELLA: No, Stanley, I haven't heard of the Napoleonic code and if I have, I don't see what it——

STANLEY: Let me enlighten you on a point or two, baby.

STELLA: Yes?

STANLEY: In the state of Louisiana we have the Napoleonic code according to which what belongs to the wife belongs to the husband and vice versa. For instance if I had a piece of property, or you had a piece of property——

STELLA: My head is swimming!

STANLEY: All right. I'll wait till she gets through soaking in a hot tub and then I'll inquire if *she* is acquainted with the Napoleonic code. It looks to me like you have been swindled, baby, and when you're swindled under the Napoleonic code I'm swindled *too*. And I don't like to be *swindled*.

STELLA: There's plenty of time to ask her questions later but if you do now she'll go to pieces again. I don't understand what happened to Belle Reve but you don't know how ridiculous you are being when you suggest that my sister or I or anyone of our family could have perpetrated a swindle on anyone else.

STANLEY: Then where's the money if the place was sold?

STELLA: Not sold—*lost, lost*!

He stalks into bedroom, and she follows him.

Stanley!

He pulls open the wardrobe trunk standing in middle of room and jerks out an armful of dresses.

STANLEY: Open your eyes to this stuff! You think she got them out of a teacher's pay?

STELLA: Hush!

STANLEY: Look at these feathers and furs that she come here to preen herself in! What's this here? A solid-gold dress, I believe! And this one! What is these here? Fox-pieces! [*He blows on them.*] Genuine fox fur-pieces, a half a mile long! Where are your fox-pieces, Stella? Bushy snow-white ones, no less! Where are your white fox-pieces.

STELLA: Those are inexpensive summer furs that Blanche has had a long time.

STANLEY: I got an acquaintance who deals in this sort of merchandise. I'll have him in here to appraise it. I'm willing to bet you there's thousands of dollars invested in this stuff here!

STELLA: Don't be such an idiot, Stanley!

He hurls the furs to the daybed. Then he jerks open small drawer in the trunk and pulls up a fist-full of costume jewellery.

STANLEY: And what have we here? The treasure chest of a pirate!

STELLA: Oh, Stanley!

STANLEY: Pearls! Ropes of them! What is this sister of yours, a deep-sea diver who brings up sunken treasures? Or is she the champion safe-cracker of all time! Bracelets of solid gold, too! Where are your pearls and gold bracelets?

STELLA: Shhh! Be still, Stanley!

STANLEY: And diamonds! A crown for an empress!

STELLA: A rhinestone tiara she wore to a costume ball.

STANLEY: What's rhinestone?

STELLA: Next door to glass.

STANLEY: Are you kidding? I have an acquaintance that works in a jewellery store. I'll have him in here to make an appraisal of this. Here's your plantation, or what was left of it, here!

STELLA: You have no idea how stupid and horrid you're being! Now close that trunk before she comes out of the bathroom!

He kicks the trunk partly closed and sits on the kitchen table.

STANLEY: The Kowalskis and the DuBois have different notions.

STELLA [*angrily*]: Indeed they have, thank heavens!—*I'm* going outside. [*She snatches up her white hat and gloves and crosses to the outside door.*] You come out with me while Blanche is getting dressed.

STANLEY: Since when do you give me orders?

STELLA: Are you going to stay here and insult her?

STANLEY: You're damn tootin' I'm going to stay here.

STELLA *goes out on the porch.* BLANCHE *comes out of the bathroom in a red satin robe.*

BLANCHE [*airily*]: Hello, Stanley! Here I am, all freshly bathed and scented, and feeling like a brand new human being!

He lights a cigarette.

STANLEY: That's good.

BLANCHE [*drawing the curtains at the windows*]: Excuse me while I slip on my pretty new dress!!

STANLEY: Go right ahead, Blanche.

She closes the drapes between the rooms.

BLANCHE: I understand there's to be a little card party to which we ladies are cordially *not* invited.

STANLEY [*ominously*]: Yeah?

BLANCHE *throws off her robe and slips into a flowered print dress.*

BLANCHE: Where's Stella?

STANLEY: Out on the porch.

BLANCHE: I'm going to ask a favour of you in a moment.

STANLEY: What could that be, I wonder?

BLANCHE: Some buttons in back! You may enter!

He crosses through drapes with a smouldering look.

How do I look?

STANLEY: You look all right.

BLANCHE: Many thanks! Now the buttons!

STANLEY: I can't do nothing with them.

BLANCHE: You men with your big clumsy fingers. May I have a drag on your cig?

STANLEY: Have one for yourself.

BLANCHE: Why, thanks! . . . It looks like my trunk has exploded.

STANLEY: Me an' Stella were helping you unpack.

BLANCHE: Well, you certainly did a fast and thorough job of it!

STANLEY: It looks like you raided some stylish shops in Paris.

BLANCHE: Ha-ha! Yes—clothes are my passion!

STANLEY: What does it cost for a string of fur-pieces like that?

BLANCHE: Why, those were a tribute from an admirer of mine!

STANLEY: He must have had a lot of—admiration!

BLANCHE: Oh, in my youth I excited some admiration. But look at me now! [*She smiles at him radiantly.*] Would you think it possible that I was once considered to be—attractive?

STANLEY: Your looks are okay.

BLANCHE: I was fishing for a compliment, Stanley.

STANLEY: I don't go in for that stuff.

BLANCHE: What—stuff?

STANLEY: Compliments to women about their looks. I never met a woman that didn't know if she was good-looking or not without being told, and some of them give themselves credit for more than they've got. I once went out with a doll who said to me, "I am the glamorous type, I am the glamorous type!" I said, "So what?"

BLANCHE: And what did she say then?

STANLEY: She didn't say nothing. That shut her up like a clam.

BLANCHE: Did it end the romance?

STANLEY: It ended the conversation—that was all. Some men are took in by this Hollywood glamour stuff and some men are not.

BLANCHE: I'm sure you belong in the second category.

STANLEY: That's right.

BLANCHE: I cannot imagine any witch of a woman casting a spell over you.

STANLEY: That's—right.

BLANCHE: You're simple, straightforward and honest, a little bit on the primitive side I should think. To interest you a woman would have to—— [*She pauses with an indefinite gesture.*]

STANLEY [*slowly*]: Lay . . . her cards on the table.

BLANCHE [*smiling*]: Yes—yes—cards on the table. . . . Well, life is too full of evasions and ambiguities, I think. I like an artist who paints in strong, bold colours, primary colours. I don't like pinks and creams and I never cared for wishy-washy people. That was why, when you walked in here last night, I said to myself—"My sister has married a man!"—Of course that was all that I could tell about you.

STANLEY [*booming*]: Now let's cut the re-bop!

BLANCHE [*pressing hands to her ears*]: Ouuuuu!

STELLA [*calling from the steps*]: Stanley! You come out here and let Blanche finish dressing!

BLANCHE: I'm through dressing, honey.

STELLA: Well, you come out, then.

STANLEY: Your sister and I are having a little talk.

BLANCHE [*lightly*]: Honey, do me a favour. Run to the drug-store and get me a lemon-coke with plenty of chipped ice in it!—Will you do that for me, Sweetie?

STELLA [*uncertainly*]: Yes. [*She goes around the corner of the building.*]

BLANCHE: The poor thing was out there listening to us, and I have an idea she doesn't understand you as well as I do. . . . All right; now, Mr. Kowalski, let us proceed without any more double-talk. I'm ready to answer all questions. I've nothing to hide. What is it?

STANLEY: There is such a thing in this State of Louisiana as the Napoleonic code, according to which whatever belongs to my wife is also mine—and vice versa.

BLANCHE: My, but you have an impressive judicial air!

She sprays herself with her atomizer; then playfully sprays him with it. He seizes the atomizer and slams it down on the dresser. She throws back her head and laughs.

STANLEY: If I didn't know that you was my wife's sister I'd get ideas about you!

BLANCHE: Such as what?

STANLEY: Don't play so dumb. You know what!—Where's the papers?

BLANCHE: Papers?

STANLEY: Papers! That stuff people write on!

BLANCHE: Oh, papers, papers! Ha-ha! The first anniversary gift, all kinds of papers!

STANLEY: I'm talking of legal papers. Connected with the plantation.

BLANCHE: There *were* some papers.

STANLEY: You mean they're no longer existing?

BLANCHE: They probably are, somewhere.

STANLEY: But not in the trunk.

BLANCHE: Everything that I own is in that trunk.

STANLEY: Then why don't we have a look for them? [*He crosses to the trunk, shoves it roughly open and begins to open compartments.*]

BLANCHE: What in the name of heaven are you thinking of! What's in the back of that little boy's mind of yours? That I am absconding with something, attempting some kind of treachery on my sister? —Let me do that! It will be faster and simpler. . . . [*She crosses to the trunk and takes out a box.*] I keep my papers mostly in this tin box. [*She opens it.*]

STANLEY: What's them underneath? [*He indicates another sheaf of paper.*]

BLANCHE: These are love-letters, yellowing with antiquity, all from one boy. [*He snatches them up. She speaks fiercely.*] Give those back to me!

STANLEY: I'll have a look at them first!

BLANCHE: The touch of your hands insults them!

STANLEY: Don't pull that stuff!

He rips off the ribbon and starts to examine them. BLANCHE snatches them from him, and they cascade to the floor.

BLANCHE: Now that you've touched them I'll burn them!

STANLEY [*staring, baffled*]: What in hell are they?

BLANCHE [*on the floor gathering them up*]: Poems a dead boy wrote. I hurt him the way that you would like to hurt me, but you can't! I'm not young and vulnerable any more. But my young husband was and I—never mind about that! Just give them back to me!

STANLEY: What do you mean by saying you'll have to burn them?

BLANCHE: I'm sorry, I must have lost my head for a moment. Everyone has something he won't let others touch because of their —intimate nature. . . .

> *She now seems faint with exhaustion and she sits down with the strong box and puts on a pair of glasses and goes methodically through a large stack of papers.*

Ambler & Ambler. Hmmmmm. . . . Crabtree. . . . More Ambler & Ambler.

STANLEY: What is Ambler & Ambler?

BLANCHE: A firm that made loans on the place.

STANLEY: Then it *was* lost on a mortgage?

BLANCHE [*touching her forehead*]: That must've been what happened.

STANLEY: I don't want no ifs, ands or buts! What's all the rest of them papers?

> *She hands him the entire box. He carries it to the table and starts to examine the papers.*

BLANCHE [*picking up a large envelope containing more papers*]: There are thousands of papers, stretching back over hundreds of years, affecting Belle Reve as, piece by piece, our improvident grandfathers and father and uncles and brothers exchanged the land for their epic fornications—to put it plainly! [*She removes her glasses with an exhausted laugh.*] Till finally all that was left—and Stella can verify that!—was the house itself and about twenty acres of ground, including a graveyard, to which now all but Stella and I have retreated. [*She pours the contents of the envelope on the table.*] Here all of them are, all papers! I hereby endow you with them! Take them, peruse them—commit them to memory, even! I think it's wonderfully fitting that Belle Reve should finally be this bunch of old papers in your big, capable hands! . . . I wonder if Stella's come back with my lemon-coke. . . .

> *She leans back and closes her eyes.*

STANLEY: I have a lawyer acquaintance who will study these out.

BLANCHE: Present them to him with a box of aspirin tablets.

STANLEY [*becoming somewhat sheepish*]: You see, under the Napoleonic code—a man has to take an interest in his wife's affairs—especially now that she's going to have a baby.

> BLANCHE *opens her eyes. The "blue piano" sounds louder.*

BLANCHE: Stella? Stella going to have a baby? [*Dreamily.*] I didn't know she was going to have a baby!

> *She gets up and crosses to the outside door. Stella appears around the corner with a carton from the drug-store.*
> *Stanley goes into the bedroom with the envelope and the box. The inner rooms fade to darkness and the outside wall of the house is visible.*
> BLANCHE *meets* STELLA *at the foot of the steps to the sidewalk.*

BLANCHE: Stella, Stella for Star! How lovely to have a baby! [*She embraces her sister.* STELLA *returns the embrace with a convulsive sob.* BLANCHE *speaks softly.*] Everything is all right; we thrashed it out. I feel a bit shaky, but I think I handled it nicely. I laughed and treated it all as a joke, called him a little boy and laughed—and flirted! Yes—I was flirting with your husband, Stella!

> STEVE *and* PABLO *appear carrying a case of beer.*

The guests are gathering for the poker party.

> *The two men pass between them, and with a short, curious stare at* BLANCHE, *they enter the house.*

STELLA: I'm sorry he did that to you.

BLANCHE: He's just not the sort that goes for jasmine perfume! But maybe he's what we need to mix with our blood now that we've lost Belle Reve and have to go on without Belle Reve to protect us. . . . How pretty the sky is! I ought to go there on a rocket that never comes down.

> *A* TAMALE VENDOR *calls out as he rounds the corner.*

VENDOR: Red hots! Red hots!

> BLANCHE *utters a sharp, frightened cry and shrinks away; then she laughs breathlessly again.*

BLANCHE: Which way do we—go now—Stella?

VENDOR: Re-e-d ho-o-ot!

BLANCHE: The blind are—leading the blind!

> *They disappear around the corner, BLANCHE'S desperate laughter ringing out once more.*
> *Then there is a bellowing laugh from the interior of the flat.*
> *Then the "blue piano" and the hot trumpet sound louder.*

SCENE III

The Poker Night.
There is a picture of Van Gogh's of a billiard-parlour at night. The kitchen now suggests that sort of lurid nocturnal brilliance, the raw colours of childhood's spectrum. Over the yellow linoleum of the kitchen table hangs an electric bulb with a vivid green glass shade. The poker players—STANLEY, STEVE, MITCH and PABLO—wear coloured shirts, solid blues, a purple, a red-and-white check, a light green, and they are men at the peak of their physical manhood, as coarse and direct and powerful as the primary colours. There are vivid slices of watermelon on the table, whisky bottles and glasses. The bedroom is relatively dim with only the light that spills between the portières and through the wide window on the street.

> *For a moment there is absorbed silence as a hand is dealt.*

STEVE: Anything wild this deal?

PABLO: One-eyed jacks are wild.

STEVE: Give me two cards.

PABLO: You, Mitch?

MITCH: I'm out.

PABLO: One.

MITCH: Anyone want a shot?

STANLEY: Yeah. Me.

PABLO: Why don't somebody go to the Chinaman's and bring back a load of chop suey?

STANLEY: When I'm losing you want to eat! Ante up! Openers? Openers! Get off the table, Mitch. Nothing belongs on a poker table but cards, chips and whisky.

> *He lurches up and tosses some watermelon rinds to the floor.*

MITCH: Kind of on your high horse, ain't you?

STANLEY: How many?

STEVE: Give me three.

STANLEY: One.

MITCH: I'm out again. I oughta go home pretty soon.

STANLEY: Shut up.

MITCH: I gotta sick mother. She don't go to sleep until I come in at night.

STANLEY: Then why don't you stay home with her?

MITCH: She says to go out, so I go, but I don't enjoy it. All the while I keep wondering how she is.

STANLEY: Aw, for God's sake, go home, then!

PABLO: What've you got?

STEVE: Spade flush.

MITCH: You all are married. But I'll be alone when she goes.— I'm going to the bathroom.

STANLEY: Hurry back and we'll fix you a sugar-tit.

MITCH: Aw, lay off. [*He crosses through the bedroom into the bathroom.*]

STEVE [*dealing a hand*]: Seven card stud. [*Telling his joke as he deals.*] This ole nigger is out in back of his house sittin' down th'owing corn to the chickens when all at once he hears a loud cackle and this young hen comes lickety split around the side of the house with the rooster right behind her and gaining on her fast.

STANLEY [*impatient with the story*]: Deal!

STEVE: But when the rooster catches sight of the nigger th'owing the corn he puts on the brakes and lets the hen get away and starts pecking corn. And the old nigger says, "Lord God, I hopes I never gits *that* hongry!"

> STEVE *and* PABLO *laugh. The sisters appear around the corner of the building.*

STELLA: The game is still going on.

BLANCHE: How do I look?

STELLA: Lovely, Blanche.

BLANCHE: I feel so hot and frazzled. Wait till I powder before you open the door. Do I look done in?

STELLA: Why no. You are as fresh as a daisy.

BLANCHE: One that's been picked a few days.

> STELLA *opens the door and they enter.*

STELLA: Well, well, well. I see you boys are still at it!

STANLEY: Where you been?

STELLA: Blanche and I took in a show. Blanche, this is Mr. Gonzales and Mr. Hubbel.

BLANCHE: Please don't get up.

STANLEY: Nobody's going to get up, so don't be worried.

STELLA: How much longer is this game going to continue?

STANLEY: Till we get ready to quit.

BLANCHE: Poker is so fascinating. Could I kibitz?

STANLEY: You could not. Why don't you women go up and sit with Eunice?

STELLA: Because it is nearly two-thirty. [BLANCHE *crosses into the bedroom and partially closes the portières.*] Couldn't you call it quits after one more hand?

A chair scrapes. STANLEY *gives a loud whack of his hand on her thigh.*

STELLA [*sharply*]: That's not fun, Stanley.

The men laugh. STELLA *goes into the bedroom.*

STELLA: It makes me so mad when he does that in front of people.

BLANCHE: I think I will bathe.

STELLA: Again?

BLANCHE: My nerves are in knots. Is the bathroom occupied?

STELLA: I don't know.

BLANCHE *knocks.* MITCH *opens the door and comes out, still wiping his hands on a towel.*

BLANCHE: Oh!—good evening.

MITCH: Hello. [*He stares at her.*]

STELLA: Blanche, this is Harold Mitchell. My sister, Blanche DuBois.

MITCH [*with awkward courtesy*]: How do you do, Miss DuBois.

STELLA: How is your mother now, Mitch?

MITCH: About the same, thanks. She appreciated your sending over that custard.—Excuse me, please.

He crosses slowly back into the kitchen, glancing back at BLANCHE *and coughing a little shyly. He realizes he still has the towel in his hands and with an embarrassed laugh hands it to* STELLA. BLANCHE *looks after him with a certain interest.*

BLANCHE: That one seems—superior to the others.

STELLA: Yes, he is.

BLANCHE: I thought he had a sort of sensitive look.

STELLA: His mother is sick.
BLANCHE: Is he married?
STELLA: No.
BLANCHE: Is he a wolf?
STELLA: Why, Blanche! [BLANCHE *laughs.*] I don't think he would be.
BLANCHE: What does—what does he do?

She is unbuttoning her blouse.

STELLA: He's on the precision bench in the spare parts department. At the plant Stanley travels for.
BLANCHE: Is that something much?
STELLA: No. Stanley's the only one of his crowd that's likely to get anywhere.
BLANCHE: What makes you think Stanley will?
STELLA: Look at him.
BLANCHE: I've looked at him.
STELLA: Then you should know.
BLANCHE: I'm sorry, but I haven't noticed the stamp of genius even on Stanley's forehead.

She takes off the blouse and stands in her pink silk brassière and white skirt in the light through the portières. The game has continued in undertones.

STELLA: It isn't on his forehead and it isn't genius.
BLANCHE: Oh. Well, what is it, and where? I would like to know.
STELLA: It's a drive that he has. You're standing in the light, Blanche!
BLANCHE: Oh, am I!

She moves out of the yellow streak of light. STELLA *has removed her dress and put on a light blue satin kimono.*

STELLA [*with girlish laughter*]: You ought to see their wives.
BLANCHE [*laughingly*]: I can imagine. Big, beefy things, I suppose.
STELLA: You know that one upstairs? [*More laughter.*] One time [*laughing*] the plaster—[*laughing*] cracked——
STANLEY: You hens cut out that conversation in there!
STELLA: You can't hear us.
STANLEY: Well, you can hear me and I said to hush up!
STELLA: This is my house and I'll talk as much as I want to!
BLANCHE: Stella, don't start a row.
STELLA: He's half drunk!—I'll be out in a minute

She goes into the bathroom. BLANCHE *rises and crosses leisurely to a small white radio and turns it on.*

STANLEY: Awright, Mitch, you in?

MITCH: What? Oh!—No, I'm out!

BLANCHE moves back into the streak of light. She raises her arms and stretches, as she moves indolently back to the chair.
Rhumba music comes over the radio. MITCH *rises at the table.*

STANLEY: Who turned that on in there?

BLANCHE: I did. Do you mind?

STANLEY: Turn it off!

STEVE: Aw, let the girls have their music.

PABLO: Sure, that's good, leave it on!

STEVE: Sounds like Xavier Cugat!

STANLEY jumps up and, crossing to the radio, turns it off. He stops short at sight of BLANCHE in the chair. She returns his look without flinching. Then he sits again at the poker table.
Two of the men have started arguing hotly.

STEVE: I didn't hear you name it.

PABLO: Didn't I name it, Mitch?

MITCH: I wasn't listenin'.

PABLO: What were you doing, then?

STANLEY: He was looking through them drapes. [*He jumps up and jerks roughly at curtains to close them.*] Now deal the hand over again and let's play cards or quit. Some people get ants when they win.

MITCH rises as STANLEY returns to his seat.

STANLEY [*yelling*]: Sit down!

MITCH: I'm going to the "head". Deal me out.

PABLO: Sure he's got ants now. Seven five-dollar bills in his pants pocket folded up tight as spitballs.

STEVE: Tomorrow you'll see him at the cashier's window getting them changed into quarters.

STANLEY: And when he goes home he'll deposit them one by one in a piggy bank his mother give him for Christmas [*Dealing.*] This game is Spit in the Ocean.

MITCH laughs uncomfortably and continues through the portières. He stops just inside.

BLANCHE [*softly*]: Hello! The Little Boys' Room is busy right now.

MITCH: We've—been drinking beer.

BLANCHE: I hate beer.

MITCH: It's—a hot weather drink.

BLANCHE: Oh, I don't think so; it always makes me warmer. Have
you got any cigs? [*She has slipped on the dark red satin wrapper.*]

MITCH: Sure.

BLANCHE: What kind are they?

MITCH: Luckies.

BLANCHE: Oh, good. What a pretty case. Silver?

MITCH: Yes. Yes; read the inscription.

BLANCHE: Oh, is there an inscription? I can't make it out. [*He
strikes a match and moves closer.*] Oh! [*reading with feigned difficulty*]
        "And if God choose,
            I shall but love thee better—after—death!"
Why, that's from my favourite sonnet by Mrs. Browning!

MITCH: You know it?

BLANCHE: Certainly I do!

MITCH: There's a story connected with that inscription.

BLANCHE: It sounds like a romance.

MITCH: A pretty sad one.

BLANCHE: Oh?

MITCH: The girl's dead now.

BLANCHE [*in a tone of deep sympathy*]: Oh!

MITCH: She knew she was dying when she give me this. A very
strange girl, very sweet—very!

BLANCHE: She must have been fond of you. Sick people have such
deep, sincere attachments.

MITCH: That's right, they certainly do.

BLANCHE: Sorrow makes for sincerity, I think.

MITCH: It sure brings it out in people.

BLANCHE: The little there is belongs to people who have experienced
some sorrow.

MITCH: I believe you are right about that.

BLANCHE: I'm positive that I am. Show me a person who hasn't
known any sorrow and I'll show you a shuperficial—— Listen to
me! My tongue is a little—thick! You boys are responsible for it.
The show let out at eleven and we couldn't come home on account
of the poker game so we had to go somewhere and drink. I'm not
accustomed to having more than one drink. Two is the limit—
and *three*! [*She laughs.*] Tonig ht I had three.

STANLEY: Mitch!

MITCH: Deal me out. I'm talking to Miss——

BLANCHE: DuBois.

MITCH: Miss DuBois?

BLANCHE: It's a French name. It means woods and Blanche means white, so the two together mean white woods. Like an orchard in spring! You can remember it by that.

MITCH: You're French?

BLANCHE: We are French by extraction. Our first American ancestors were French Huguenots.

MITCH: You are Stella's sister, are you not?

BLANCHE: Yes, Stella is my precious little sister. I call her little in spite of the fact she's somewhat older than I. Just slightly. Less than a year. Will you do something for me?

MITCH: Sure. What?

BLANCHE: I bought this adorable little coloured paper lantern at a Chinese shop on Bourbon. Put it over the light bulb! Will you, please?

MITCH: Be glad to.

BLANCHE: I can't stand a naked light bulb, any more than I can a rude remark or a vulgar action.

MITCH [adjusting the lantern]: I guess we strike you as being a pretty rough bunch.

BLANCHE: I'm very adaptable—to circumstances.

MITCH: Well, that's a good thing to be. You are visiting Stanley and Stella?

BLANCHE: Stella hasn't been so well lately, and I came down to help her for a while. She's very run down.

MITCH: You're not——?

BLANCHE: Married? No, no. I'm an old maid schoolteacher!

MITCH: You may teach school but you're certainly not an old maid.

BLANCHE: Thank you, sir! I appreciate your gallantry!

MITCH: So you are in the teaching profession?

BLANCHE: Yes. Ah, yes . . .

MITCH: Grade school or high school or——

STANLEY [bellowing]: Mitch!

MITCH: Coming!

BLANCHE: Gracious, what lung-power! . . . I teach high school. In Laurel.

MITCH: What do you teach? What subject?

BLANCHE: Guess!

MITCH: I bet you teach art or music? [BLANCHE *laughs delicately.*]
Of course I could be wrong. You might teach arithmetic.

BLANCHE: Never arithmetic, sir; never arithmetic! [*with a laugh*]
I don't even know my multiplication tables! No, I have the misfortune of being an English instructor. I attempt to instil a bunch
of bobby-soxers and drug-store Romeos with reverence for Hawthorne and Whitman and Poe!

MITCH: I guess that some of them are more interested in other
things.

BLANCHE: How very right you are! Their literary heritage is not
what most of them treasure above all else! But they're sweet
things! And in the spring, it's touching to notice them making
their first discovery of love! As if nobody had ever known it
before!

> *The bathroom door opens and* STELLA *comes out.* BLANCHE *con-*
> *tinues talking to* MITCH.

Oh! Have you finished? Wait—I'll turn on the radio.

> *She turns the knobs on the radio and it begins to play* "*Wien, Wien,*
> *nur du allein.*" BLANCHE *waltzes to the music with romantic gestures.*
> MITCH *is delighted and moves in awkward imitation like a dancing*
> *bear.*
> STANLEY *stalks fiercely through the portières into the bedroom.*
> *He crosses to the small white radio and snatches it off the table. With*
> *a shouted oath, he tosses the instrument out of the window.*

STELLA: *Drunk—drunk—animal thing, you!* [*She rushes through to*
the poker table.] All of you—please go home! If any of you have
one spark of decency in you——

BLANCHE: [*wildly*]: Stella, watch out, he's——

> STANLEY *charges after* STELLA.

MEN [*feebly*]: Take it easy, Stanley. Easy, fellow.—Let's all——

STELLA: You lay your hands on me and I'll——

> *She backs out of sight. He advances and disappears. There is the*
> *sound of a blow.* STELLA *cries out.* BLANCHE *screams and runs*
> *into the kitchen. The men rush forward and there is grappling and*
> *cursing. Something is overturned with a crash.*

BLANCHE [*shrilly*]: My sister is going to have a baby!

MITCH: This is terrible.

BLANCHE: Lunacy, absolute lunacy!

MITCH: Get him in here, men.

> STANLEY *is forced, pinioned by the two men, into the bedroom. He nearly throws them off. Then all at once he subsides and is limp in their grasp.*
> *They speak quietly and lovingly to him and he leans his face on one of their shoulders.*

STELLA [*in a high, unnatural voice, out of sight*]: I want to go away, I want to go away!

MITCH: Poker shouldn't be played in a house with women.

> BLANCHE *rushes into the bedroom.*

BLANCHE: I want my sister's clothes! We'll go to that woman's upstairs!

MITCH: Where is the clothes?

BLANCHE [*opening the closet*]: I've got them! [*She rushes through to* STELLA.] Stella, Stella, precious! Dear, dear little sister, don't be afraid!

> With her arms around STELLA, BLANCHE *guides her to the outside doors and upstairs.*

STANLEY [*dully*]: What's the matter; what's happened?

MITCH: You just blew your top, Stan.

PABLO: He's okay, now.

STEVE: Sure, my boy's okay!

MITCH: Put him on the bed and get a wet towel.

PABLO: I think coffee would do him a world of good, now.

STANLEY [*thickly*]: I want water.

MITCH: Put him under the shower!

> *The men talk quietly as they lead him to the bathroom.*

STANLEY: Let go of me, you sons of bitches!

> *Sounds of blows are heard. The water goes on full tilt.*

STEVE: Let's get quick out of here!

> *They rush to the poker table and sweep up their winnings on their way out.*

MITCH [*sadly but firmly*]: Poker should not be played in a house with women.

The door closes on them and the place is still. The Negro entertainers in the bar around the corner play "Paper Doll" slow and blue. After a moment STANLEY *comes out of the bathroom dripping water and still in his clinging wet polka dot drawers.*

STANLEY: Stella! [*There is a pause.*] My baby doll's left me!

He breaks into sobs. Then he goes to the phone and dials, still shudder-ing with sobs.

Eunice? I want my baby! [*He waits a moment; then he hangs up and dials again.*] Eunice! I'll keep on ringin' until I talk with my baby!

An indistinguishable shrill voice is heard. He hurls phone to floor. Dissonant brass and piano sounds as the rooms dim out to darkness and the outer walls appear in the night light. The "blue piano" plays for a brief interval.
Finally, STANLEY *stumbles half-dressed out to the porch and down the wooden steps to the pavement before the building. There he throws back his head like a baying hound and bellows his wife's name: "Stella! Stella, sweetheart! Stella!"*

STANLEY: Stell-*lahhhhh!*
EUNICE [*calling down from the door of her upper apartment*]: Quit that howling out there an' go back to bed!
STANLEY: I want my baby down here. Stella, Stella!
EUNICE: She ain't comin' down so you quit! Or you'll git th' law on you!
STANLEY: Stella!
EUNICE: You can't beat on a woman an' then call 'er back! She won't come! And her goin' t' have a baby! . . . You stinker! You whelp of a Polack, you! I hope they do haul you in and turn the fire hose on you, same as the last time!
STANLEY [*humbly*]: Eunice, I want my girl to come down with me!
EUNICE: Hah! [*She slams her door.*]
STANLEY [*with heaven-splitting violence*]: *STELL-LAHHHHHH!*

The low-tone clarinet moans. The door upstairs opens again. STELLA *slips down the rickety stairs in her robe. Her eyes are glistening with tears and her hair loose about her throat and shoulders. They stare at each other. Then they come together with low, animal moans. He falls to his knees on the steps and presses his face to her belly, curving a little with maternity. Her eyes go blind with tenderness as she catches his head and raises him level with her. He snatches the screen door open and lifts her off her feet and bears her into the dark flat.*

BLANCHE comes out on the upper landing in her robe and slips fearfully down the steps.

BLANCHE: Where is my little sister? Stella? Stella?

She stops before the dark entrance of her sister's flat. Then catches her breath as if struck. She rushes down to the walk before the house. She looks right and left as if for sanctuary.

The music fades away. MITCH appears from around the corner.

MITCH: Miss DuBois?

BLANCHE: Oh!

MITCH: All quiet on the Potomac now?

BLANCHE: She ran downstairs and went back in there with him.

MITCH: Sure she did.

BLANCHE: I'm terrified!

MITCH: Ho-ho! There's nothing to be scared of. They're crazy about each other.

BLANCHE: I'm not used to such——

MITCH: Naw, it's a shame this had to happen when you just got here. But don't take it serious.

BLANCHE: Violence! Is so——

MITCH: Set down on the steps and have a cigarette with me.

BLANCHE: I'm not properly dressed.

MITCH: That's don't make no difference in the Quarter.

BLANCHE: Such a pretty silver case.

MITCH: I showed you the inscription, didn't I?

BLANCHE: Yes. [*During the pause, she looks up at the sky.*] There's so much—so much confusion in the world. . . . [*He coughs diffidently.*] Thank you for being so kind! I need kindness now.

SCENE IV

It is early the following morning. There is a confusion of street cries like a choral chant.

STELLA *is lying down in the bedroom. Her face is serene in the early morning sunlight. One hand rests on her belly, rounding slightly with new maternity. From the other dangles a book of coloured comics. Her*

*eyes and lips have that almost narcotized tranquillity that is in the
faces of Eastern idols.*

*The table is sloppy with remains of breakfast and the debris of the
preceding night, and* STANLEY'S *gaudy pyjamas lie across the thres-
hold of the bathroom. The outside door is slightly ajar on a sky of
summer brilliance.*

BLANCHE *appears at this door. She has spent a sleepless night and
her appearance entirely contrasts with* STELLA'S. *She presses her
knuckles nervously to her lips as she looks through the door, before
entering.*

BLANCHE: Stella?

STELLA [*stirring lazily*]: Hmmh?

> BLANCHE *utters a moaning cry and runs into the bedroom, throwing
> herself down beside* STELLA *in a rush of hysterical tenderness.*

BLANCHE: Baby, my baby sister!

STELLA [*drawing away from her*]: Blanche, what is the matter with
you?

> BLANCHE *straightens up slowly and stands beside the bed looking down
> at her sister with knuckles pressed to her lips.*

BLANCHE: He's left?

STELLA: Stan? Yes.

BLANCHE: Will he be back?

STELLA: He's gone to get the car greased. Why?

BLANCHE: Why! I've been half crazy, Stella! When I found out
you'd been insane enough to come back in here after what happened
—I started to rush in after you!

STELLA: I'm glad you didn't.

BLANCHE: What were you thinking of? [STELLA *makes an indefinite
gesture.*] Answer me! What? What?

STELLA: Please, Blanche! Sit down and stop yelling.

BLANCHE: All right, Stella. I will repeat the question quietly now.
How could you come back in this place last night? Why, you must
have slept with him!

> STELLA *gets up in a calm and leisurely way.*

STELLA: Blanche, I'd forgotten how excitable you are. You're
making much too much fuss about this.

BLANCHE: Am I?

STELLA: Yes, you are, Blanche. I know how it must have seemed

to you and I'm awful sorry it had to happen, but it wasn't anything
as serious as you seem to take it. In the first place, when men are
drinking and playing poker anything can happen. It's always a
powder-keg. He didn't know what he was doing. . . . He was as
good as a lamb when I came back and he's really very, very ashamed
of himself.

BLANCHE: And that—that makes it all right?

STELLA: No, it isn't all right for anybody to make such a terrible row,
but—people do sometimes. Stanley's always smashed things.
Why, on our wedding night—soon as we came in here—he snatched
off one of my slippers and rushed about the place smashing the light-
bulbs with it.

BLANCHE: He did—*what*?

STELLA: He smashed all the light-bulbs with the heel of my slipper!
[*She laughs.*]

BLANCHE: And you—you *let* him? Didn't *run*, didn't *scream*?

STELLA: I was—sort of—thrilled by it. [*She waits for a moment.*]
Eunice and you had breakfast?

BLANCHE: Do you suppose I wanted any breakfast?

STELLA: There's some coffee left on the stove.

BLANCHE: You're so—matter of fact about it, Stella.

STELLA: What other can I be? He's taken the radio to get it fixed.
It didn't land on the pavement so only one tube was smashed.

BLANCHE: And you are standing there smiling!

STELLA: What do you want me to do?

BLANCHE: Pull yourself together and face the facts.

STELLA: What are they, in your opinion?

BLANCHE: In my opinion? You're married to a madman!

STELLA: No!

BLANCHE: Yes, you are, your fix is worse than mine is! Only you're
not being sensible about it. I'm going to *do* something. Get hold of
myself and make myself a new life!

STELLA: Yes?

BLANCHE: But you've given in. And that isn't right, you're not old!
You can get out.

STELLA [*slowly and emphatically*]: I'm not in anything I want to get
out of.

BLANCHE [*incredulously*]: What—Stella?

STELLA: I said I am not in anything that I have a desire to get out of.
Look at the mess in this room! And those empty bottles! They went
through two cases last night! He promised this morning that he

was going to quit having these poker parties, but you know how
long such a promise is going to keep. Oh, well, it's his pleasure, like
mine is movies and bridge. People have got to tolerate each other's
habits, I guess.

BLANCHE: I don't understand you. [STELLA *turns toward her.*] I
don't understand your indifference. Is this a Chinese philosophy
you've—cultivated?

STELLA: Is what—what?

BLANCHE: This—shuffling about and mumbling—"One tube
smashed—beer-bottles—mess in the kitchen"—as if nothing out of
the ordinary has happened! [STELLA *laughs uncertainly and picking
up the broom, twirls it in her hands.*]

BLANCHE: Are you deliberately shaking that thing in my face?

STELLA: No.

BLANCHE: Stop it. Let go of that broom. I won't have you cleaning
up for him!

STELLA: Then who's going to do it? Are you?

BLANCHE: I? I!

STELLA: No, I didn't think so.

BLANCHE: Oh, let me think, if only my mind would function!
We've got to get hold of some money, that's the way out!

STELLA: I guess that money is always nice to get hold of.

BLANCHE: Listen to me. I have an idea of some kind. [*Shakily she
twists a cigarette into her holder.*] Do you remember Shep Huntleigh?
[STELLA *shakes her head.*] Of course you remember Shep Huntleigh.
I went out with him at college and wore his pin for a while. Well——

STELLA: Well?

BLANCHE: I ran into him last winter. You know I went to Miami
during the Christmas holidays?

STELLA: No.

BLANCHE: Well, I did. I took the trip as an investment, thinking
I'd meet someone with a million dollars.

STELLA: Did you?

BLANCHE: Yes. I ran into Shep Huntleigh—I ran into him on Biscayne Boulevard, on Christmas Eve, about dusk . . . getting into
his car—Cadillac convertible; must have been a block long!

STELLA: I should think it would have been—inconvenient in traffic!

BLANCHE: You've heard of oil-wells?

STELLA: Yes—remotely.

BLANCHE: He has them, all over Texas. Texas is literally spouting
gold in his pockets.

STELLA: My, my.

BLANCHE: Y'know how indifferent I am to money. I think of money in terms of what it does for you. But he could do it, he could certainly do it!

STELLA: Do what, Blanche?

BLANCHE: Why—set us up in a—shop!

STELLA: What kind of a shop?

BLANCHE: Oh, a—shop of some kind! He could do it with half what his wife throws away at the races.

STELLA: He's married?

BLANCHE: Honey, would I be here if the man weren't married? [STELLA *laughs a little.* BLANCHE *suddenly springs up and crosses to phone. She speaks shrilly.*] How do I get Western Union?—Operator! Western Union!

STELLA: That's a dial phone, honey.

BLANCHE: I can't dial, I'm too——

STELLA: Just dial O.

BLANCHE: O?

STELLA: Yes, "O" for Operator! [BLANCHE *considers a moment; then she puts the phone down.*]

BLANCHE: Give me a pencil. Where is a slip of paper? I've got to write it down first—the message, I mean . . .

She goes to the dressing-table, and grabs up a sheet of Kleenex and an eyebrow pencil for writing equipment.

Let me see now . . . [*She bites the pencil.*] "Darling Shep. Sister and I in desperate situation."

STELLA: I beg your pardon!

BLANCHE: "Sister and I in desperate situation. Will explain details later. Would you be interested in——?" [*She bites the pencil again.*] "Would you be—interested—in . . ." [*She smashes the pencil on the table and springs up.*] You never get anywhere with direct appeals!

STELLA [*with a laugh*]: Don't be so ridiculous, darling!

BLANCHE: But I'll think of something, I've *got* to think of—something! Don't, don't laugh at me, Stella! Please, please don't—I— I want you to look at the contents of my purse! Here's what's in it! [*She snatches her purse open.*] Sixty-five measly cents in coin of the realm!

STELLA [*crossing to bureau*]: Stanley doesn't give me a regular allowance, he likes to pay bills himself, but—this morning he gave me ten dollars to smooth things over. You take five of it, Blanche, and I'll keep the rest.

BLANCHE: Oh, no. No, Stella.

STELLA [*insisting*]: I know how it helps your morale just having a little pocket-money on you.

BLANCHE: No, thank you—I'll take to the streets!

STELLA: Talk sense! How did you happen to get so low on funds?

BLANCHE: Money just goes—it goes places. [*She rubs her forehead.*] Sometime today I've got to get hold of a bromo!

STELLA: I'll fix you one now.

BLANCHE: Not yet—I've got to keep thinking!

STELLA: I wish you'd just let things go, at least for a—while . . .

BLANCHE: Stella, I can't live with him! You can, he's your husband. But how could I stay here with him, after last night, with just those curtains between us?

STELLA: Blanche, you saw him at his worst last night.

BLANCHE: On the contrary, I saw him at his best! What such a man has to offer is animal force and he gave a wonderful exhibition of that! But the only way to live with such a man is to—go to bed with him! And that's your job—not mine!

STELLA: After you've rested a little, you'll see it's going to work out. You don't have to worry about anything while you're here. I mean—expenses . . .

BLANCHE: I have to plan for us both, to get us both—out!

STELLA: You take it for granted that I am in something that I want to get out of.

BLANCHE: I take it for granted that you still have sufficient memory of Belle Reve to find this place and these poker players impossible to live with.

STELLA: Well, you're taking entirely too much for granted.

BLANCHE: I can't believe you're in earnest.

STELLA: No?

BLANCHE: I understand how it happened—a little. You saw him in uniform, an officer, not here but——

STELLA: I'm not sure it would have made any difference where I saw him.

BLANCHE: Now don't say it was one of those mysterious electric things between people! If you do I'll laugh in your face.

STELLA: I am not going to say anything more at all about it!

BLANCHE: All right, then, don't!

STELLA: But there are things that happen between a man and a woman in the dark—that sort of make everything else seem—unimportant. [*Pause.*]

BLANCHE: What you are talking about is brutal desire—just—Desire!—the name of that rattle-trap street-car that bangs through the Quarter, up one old narrow street and down another . . .

STELLA: Haven't you ever ridden on that street-car?

BLANCHE: It brought me here.—Where I'm not wanted and where I'm ashamed to be . . .

STELLA: Then don't you think your superior attitude is a bit out of place?

BLANCHE: I am not being or feeling at all superior, Stella. Believe me I'm not! It's just this. This is how I look at it. A man like that is someone to go out with—once—twice—three times when the devil is in you. But live with! Have a child by?

STELLA: I have told you I love him.

BLANCHE: Then I *tremble* for you! I just—*tremble* for you. . . .

STELLA: I can't help your trembling if you insist on trembling!

There is a pause.

BLANCHE: May I—speak—*plainly*?

STELLA: Yes, do. Go ahead. As plainly as you want to.

Outside, a train approaches. They are silent till the noise subsides. They are both in the bedroom.
Under cover of the train's noise STANLEY enters from outside. He stands unseen by the women, holding some packages in his arms, and overhears their following conversation. He wears an undershirt and grease-stained seersucker pants.

BLANCHE: Well—if you'll forgive me—he's *common*!

STELLA: Why, yes, I suppose he is.

BLANCHE: Suppose! You can't have forgotten that much of our bringing up, Stella, that you just *suppose* that any part of a gentleman's in his nature! *Not one particle, no!* Oh, if he was just—*ordinary*! Just *plain*—but good and wholesome, but—*no*. There's something downright—*bestial*—about him! You're hating me saying this, aren't you?

STELLA [*coldly*]: Go on and say it all, Blanche.

BLANCHE: He acts like an animal, has an animal's habits! Eats like one, moves like one, talks like one! There's even something—sub-human—something not quite to the stage of humanity yet! Yes, something—ape-like about him, like one of those pictures

I've seen in—anthropological studies! Thousands and thousands
of years have passed him right by, and there he is—Stanley Kowalski
—survivor of the stone age! Bearing the raw meat home from the
kill in the jungle! And you—*you* here—*waiting* for him! Maybe
he'll strike you or maybe grunt and kiss you! That is, if kisses have
been discovered yet! Night falls and the other apes gather! There
in the front of the cave, all grunting like him, and swilling and
gnawing and hulking! His poker night!—you call it—this party of
apes! Somebody growls—some creature snatches at something—
the fight is on! *God!* Maybe we are a long way from being made in
God's image, but Stella—my sister—there has been *some* progress
since then! Such things as art—as poetry and music—such kinds of
new light have come into the world since then! In some kinds of
people some tenderer feelings have had some little beginning!
That we have got to make *grow*! And *cling* to, and hold as our flag!
In this dark march toward whatever it is we're approaching. . .
Don't—don't hang back with the brutes!

> *Another train passes outside.* STANLEY *hesitates, licking his lips.
> Then suddenly he turns stealthily about and withdraws through front
> door. The women are still unaware of his presence. When the train has
> passed he calls through the closed front door.*

STANLEY: Hey! Hey, Stella!
STELLA [*who has listened gravely to* BLANCHE]: Stanley!
BLANCHE: Stell, I——

> *But* STELLA *has gone to the front door.* STANLEY *enters casually
> with his packages.*

STANLEY: Hiyuh, Stella, Blanche back?
STELLA: Yes, she's back.
STANLEY: Hiyuh, Blanche. [*He grins at her.*]
STELLA: You must've got under the car.
STANLEY: Them darn mechanics at Fritz's don't know their can
   from third base!

> STELLA *has embraced him with both arms, fiercely, and full in the
> view of* BLANCHE. *He laughs and clasps her head to him. Over her
> head he grins through the curtains at* BLANCHE.
> *As the lights fade away, with a lingering brightness on their embrace,
> the music of the "blue piano" and trumpet and drums is heard.*

SCENE V

BLANCHE *is seated in the bedroom fanning herself with a palm leaf as she reads over a just completed letter. Suddenly she bursts into a peal of laughter.* STELLA *is dressing in the bedroom.*

STELLA: What are you laughing at, honey?

BLANCHE: Myself, myself, for being such a liar! I'm writing a letter to Shep. [*She picks up the letter.*] "Darling Shep. I am spending the summer on the wing, making flying visits here and there. And who knows, perhaps I shall take a sudden notion to *swoop* down on *Dallas*! How would you feel about that? Ha-ha! [*She laughs nervously and brightly, touching her throat as if actually talking to* SHEP.] Forewarned is forearmed, as they say!"—How does that sound?

STELLA: Uh-huh . . .

BLANCHE [*going on nervously*]: "Most of my sister's friends go north in the summer but some have homes on the Gulf and there has been a continued round of entertainments, teas, cocktails, and luncheons——"

A disturbance is heard upstairs at the HUBBELS' *apartment.*

STELLA [*crossing to the door*]: Eunice seems to be having some trouble with Steve.

EUNICE'S *voice shouts in terrible wrath.*

EUNICE: I heard about you and that blonde!

STEVE: That's a damn lie!

EUNICE: You ain't pulling the wool over my eyes! I wouldn't mind if you'd stay down at the Four Deuces, but you always going up.

STEVE: Who ever seen me up?

EUNICE: I seen you chasing her 'round the balcony—I'm gonna call the vice squad!

STEVE: Don't you throw that at me!

EUNICE [*shrieking*]: You hit me! I'm gonna call the police!

A clatter of aluminium striking a wall is heard, followed by a man's angry roar, shouts and overturned furniture. There is a crash; then a relative hush.

BLANCHE [*brightly*]: Did he *kill* her?

> EUNICE *appears on the steps in daemonic disorder.*

STELLA: No! She's coming downstairs.

EUNICE: Call the police, I'm going to call the police! [*She rushes around the corner.*

STELLA [*returning from the door*]: Some of your sister's friends have stayed in the city.

> *They laugh lightly.* STANLEY *comes around the corner in his green and scarlet silk bowling shirt. He trots up the steps and bangs into the kitchen.* BLANCHE *registers his entrance with nervous gestures.*

STANLEY: What's a matter with Eun-uss?

STELLA: She and Steve had a row. Has she got the police?

STANLEY: Naw. She's gettin' a drink.

STELLA: That's much more practical!

> STEVE *comes down nursing a bruise on his forehead and looks in the door.*

STEVE: *She here?*

STANLEY: Naw, naw. At the Four Deuces.

STEVE: That hunk! [*He looks around the corner a bit timidly, then turns with affected boldness and runs after her.*]

BLANCHE: I must jot that down in my notebook. Ha-ha! I'm compiling a notebook of quaint little words and phrases I've picked up here.

STANLEY: You won't pick up nothing here you ain't heard before.

BLANCHE: Can I count on that?

STANLEY: You can count on it up to five hundred.

BLANCHE: That's a mighty high number. [*He jerks open the bureau drawer, slams it shut and throws shoes in a corner. At each noise* BLANCHE *winces slightly. Finally she speaks.*] What sign were you born under?

STANLEY [*while he is dressing*]: Sign?

BLANCHE: Astrological sign. I bet you were born under Aries. Aries people are forceful and dynamic. They dote on noise! They love to bang things around! You must have had lots of banging around in the army, and now that you're out, you make up for it by treating inanimate objects with such a fury!

> STELLA *has been going in and out of closet during this scene. Now she pops her head out of the closet.*

STELLA: Stanley was born just five minutes after Christmas.

BLANCHE: Capricorn—the Goat!

STANLEY: What sign were *you* born under?

BLANCHE: Oh, my birthday's next month, the fifteenth of September; that's under Virgo.

STANLEY: What's Virgo?

BLANCHE: Virgo is the Virgin.

STANLEY [*contemptuously*]: *Hah!* [*He advances a little as he knots his tie.*] Say, do you happen to know somebody named Shaw?

> *Her face expresses a faint shock. She reaches for the cologne bottle and dampens her handkerchief as she answers carefully.*

BLANCHE: Why, everybody knows somebody named Shaw!

STANLEY: Well, this somebody named Shaw is under the impression he met you in Laurel, but I figure he must have got you mixed up with some other party because this other party is someone he met at a hotel called the Flamingo.

> BLANCHE *laughs breathlessly as she touches the cologne-dampened handkerchief to her temples.*

BLANCHE: I'm afraid he does have me mixed up with this "other party". The Hotel Flamingo is not the sort of establishment I would dare to be seen in!

STANLEY: You know of it?

BLANCHE: Yes, I've seen it and smelled it.

STANLEY: You must've got pretty close if you could smell it.

BLANCHE: The odour of cheap perfume is penetrating.

STANLEY: That stuff you use is expensive?

BLANCHE: Twenty-five dollars an ounce! I'm nearly out. That's just a hint if you want to remember my birthday! [*She speaks lightly but her voice has a note of fear.*]

STANLEY: Shaw must've got you mixed up. He goes in and out of Laurel all the time, so he can check on it and clear up any mistake.

> *He turns away and crosses to the portières.* BLANCHE *closes her eyes as if faint. Her hand trembles as she lifts the handkerchief again to her forehead.*
> STEVE *and* EUNICE *come around corner.* STEVE'S *arm is around* EUNICE'S *shoulder and she is sobbing luxuriously and he is cooing love-words. There is a murmur of thunder as they go slowly upstairs in a tight embrace.*

STANLEY [*to* STELLA]: I'll wait for you at the Four Deuces!

STELLA: Hey! Don't I rate one kiss?

STANLEY: Not in front of your sister.

He goes out. BLANCHE *rises from her chair. She seems faint; looks about her with an expression of almost panic.*

BLANCHE: Stella! What have you heard about me?

STELLA: Huh?

BLANCHE: What have people been telling you about me?

STELLA: Telling?

BLANCHE: You haven't heard any—unkind—gossip about me?

STELLA: Why, no, Blanche, of course not!

BLANCHE: Honey, there was—a good deal of talk in Laurel.

STELLA: About *you*, Blanche?

BLANCHE: I wasn't so good the last two years or so, after Belle Reve had started to slip through my fingers.

STELLA: All of us do things we——

BLANCHE: I never was hard or self-sufficient enough. When people are soft—soft people have got to court the favour of hard ones, Stella. Have got to be seductive—put on soft colours, the colours of butterfly wings, and glow—make a little—temporary magic just in order to pay for—one night's shelter! That's why I've been —not so awf'ly good lately. I've run for protection, Stella, from under one leaky roof to another leaky roof—because it was storm —all storm, and I was—caught in the centre. . . . People don't see you—*men* don't—don't even admit your existence unless they are making love to you. And you've got to have your existence admitted by someone, if you're going to have someone's protection. And so the soft people have got to—shimmer and glow—put a —paper lantern over the light. . . . But I'm scared now—awf'ly scared. I don't know how much longer I can turn the trick. It isn't enough to be soft. You've got to be soft *and attractive.* And I—I'm fading now!

The afternoon has faded to dusk. STELLA *goes into the bedroom and turns on the light under the paper lantern. She holds a bottled soft drink in her hand.*

Have you been listening to me?

STELLA: I don't listen to you when you are being morbid! [*She advances with the bottled coke.*]

BLANCHE [*with abrupt change to gaiety*]: Is that coke for me?

STELLA: Not for anyone else!

BLANCHE: Why, you precious thing, you! Is it just coke?

STELLA [turning]: You mean you want a shot in it!

BLANCHE: Well, honey, a shot never does a coke any harm! Let me? You mustn't wait on me!

STELLA: I like to wait on you, Blanche. It makes it seem more like home. [She goes into the kitchen, finds a glass and pours a shot of whisky into it.]

BLANCHE: I have to admit I love to be waited on. . . .

> She rushes into the bedroom. STELLA goes to her with the glass. BLANCHE suddenly clutches STELLA's free hand with a moaning sound and presses the hand to her lips. STELLA is embarrassed by her show of emotion. BLANCHE speaks in a choked voice.

You're—you're—so *good* to me! And I——

STELLA: Blanche.

BLANCHE: I know, I won't! You hate me to talk sentimental. But honey, *believe* I feel things more than I *tell* you! I *won't* stay long! I won't, I *promise* I——

STELLA: Blanche!

BLANCHE [hysterically]: I won't, I promise, *I'll* go! Go *soon*! I will *really*! I *won't* hang around until he—throws me out. . . .

STELLA: Now will you stop talking foolish?

BLANCHE: Yes, honey. Watch how you pour—that fizzy stuff foams over!

> BLANCHE laughs shrilly and grabs the glass, but her hand shakes so it almost slips from her grasp. STELLA pours the coke into the glass. It foams over and spills. BLANCHE gives a piercing cry.

STELLA [shocked by the cry]: Heavens!

BLANCHE: Right on my pretty white skirt!

STELLA: Oh. . . . Use my hanky. Blot gently.

BLANCHE [slowly recovering]: I know—gently—gently . . .

STELLA: Did it stain?

BLANCHE: Not a bit. Ha-ha! Isn't that lucky? [She sits down shakily, taking a grateful drink. She holds the glass in both hands and continues to laugh a little.]

STELLA: Why did you scream like that?

BLANCHE: I don't know why I screamed! [Continuing nervously.] Mitch—Mitch is coming at seven. I guess I am just feeling nervous about our relations. [She begins to talk rapidly and breathlessly.] He hasn't gotten a thing but a goodnight kiss, that's all I have given him, Stella. I want his respect. And men don't want anything they get too easy. But on the other hand men lose interest quickly. Especially when the girl is over—thirty. They think a girl over thirty ought to—the vulgar term is—"put out." . . . And I—I'm not "putting out." Of course he—he doesn't know—I mean I haven't informed him—of my real age!

STELLA: Why are you sensitive about your age?

BLANCHE: Because of hard knocks my vanity's been given. What I mean is—he thinks I'm sort of—prim and proper, you know! [*She laughs out sharply.*] I want to *deceive* him enough to make him— want me. . . .

STELLA: Blanche, do you want *him*?

BLANCHE: I want to *rest*! I want to breathe quietly again! Yes—I *want* Mitch . . . *very badly*! Just think! If it happens! I can leave here and not be anyone's problem. . . .

STANLEY *comes around the corner with a drink under his belt.*

STANLEY [*bawling*]: Hey, Steve! Hey, Eunice! Hey, Stella!

There are joyous calls from above. Trumpet and drums are heard from around the corner.

STELLA [*kissing* BLANCHE *impulsively*]: It *will* happen!

BLANCHE [*doubtfully*]: It will?

STELLA: It *will*! [*She goes across into the kitchen, looking back at* BLANCHE.] It will, honey, *it will.* . . . But don't take another drink! [*Her voice catches as she goes out of the door to meet her husband.*]

BLANCHE *sinks faintly back in her chair with her drink.* EUNICE *shrieks with laughter and runs down the steps.* STEVE *bounds after her with goat-like screeches and chases her around corner.* STANLEY *and* STELLA *twine arms as they follow, laughing.*

Dusk settles deeper. The music from the Four Deuces is slow and blue.

BLANCHE: Ah, me, ah, me, ah, me . . .

Her eyes fall shut and the palm leaf drops from her fingers. She slaps her hand on the chair arm a couple of times; then she raises herself wearily to her feet and picks up the hand mirror.

There is a little glimmer of lightning about the building.

The NEGRO WOMAN, *cackling hysterically, swaying drunkenly, comes around the corner from the Four Deuces. At the same time, a*

Young Man enters from the opposite direction. The Negro Woman snaps her fingers before his belt.

Negro Woman: Hey! Sugar!

She says something indistinguishable. The Young Man shakes his head violently and edges hastily up the steps. He rings the bell. Blanche puts down the mirror. The Negro Woman has wandered down the street.

Blanche: Come in.

The Young Man appears through the portières. She regards him with interest.

Blanche: Well, well! What can I do for *you*?

Young Man: I'm collecting for *The Evening Star*.

Blanche: I didn't know that stars took up collections.

Young Man: It's the paper.

Blanche: I know, I was joking—feebly! Will you—have a drink?

Young Man: No, ma'am. No, thank you. I can't drink on the job.

Blanche: Oh, well, now, let's see. . . . No, I don't have a dime! I'm not the lady of the house. I'm her sister from Mississippi. I'm one of those poor relations you've heard about.

Young Man: That's all right. I'll drop by later. [*He starts to go out. She approaches a little.*]

Blanche: Hey! [*He turns back shyly. She puts a cigarette in a long holder.*] Could you give me a light? [*She crosses toward him. They meet at the door between the two rooms.*]

Young Man: Sure. [*He takes out a lighter.*] This doesn't always work.

Blanche: It's temperamental? [*It flares.*] Ah! Thank you.

Young Man: Thank *you*! [*He starts away again.*]

Blanche: Hey! [*He turns again, still more uncertainly. She goes close to him.*] What time is it?

Young Man: Fifteen of seven.

Blanche: So late? Don't you just love these long rainy afternoons in New Orleans when an hour isn't just an hour—but a little bit of Eternity dropped in your hands—and who knows what to do with it?

Young Man: Yes, ma'am.

In the ensuing pause, the "blue piano" is heard. It continues through the rest of this scene and the opening of the next. The Young Man clears his throat and looks glancingly at the door.

BLANCHE: You—uh—didn't get wet in the shower?

YOUNG MAN: No, ma'am. I stepped inside.

BLANCHE: In a drug-store? And had a soda?

YOUNG MAN: Uhhuh.

BLANCHE: Chocolate?

YOUNG MAN: No, ma'am. Cherry.

BLANCHE: Mmmm!

YOUNG MAN: A cherry soda!

BLANCHE: You make my mouth water.

YOUNG MAN: Well, I'd better be——

BLANCHE: Young man! Young, young, young, young—man! Has anyone ever told you that you look like a young prince out of the Arabian Nights?

YOUNG MAN: No, ma'am.

The YOUNG MAN *laughs uncomfortably and stands like a bashful kid.* BLANCHE *speaks softly to him.*

BLANCHE: Well, you do, honey lamb. Come here! Come on over here like I told you! I want to kiss you—just once—softly and sweetly on your mouth. [*Without waiting for him to accept, she crosses quickly to him and presses her lips to his.*] Run along now! It would be nice to keep you, but I've got to be good and keep my hands off children. Adios!

YOUNG MAN: Huh?

He stares at her a moment. She opens the door for him and blows a kiss to him as he goes down the steps with a dazed look. She stands there a little dreamily after he has disappeared. Then MITCH *appears around the corner with a bunch of roses.*

BLANCHE: Look who's coming! My Rosenkavalier! Bow to me first! Now present them.

He does so. She curtsies low.

Ahhh! Merciiii!

SCENE VI

It is about two a.m. the same night. The outer wall of the building is visible. BLANCHE *and* MITCH *come in. The utter exhaustion which only a neurasthenic personality can know is evident in* BLANCHE'S *voice and manner.* MITCH *is stolid but depressed. They have probably been out to the amusement park on Lake Pontchartrain, for* MITCH *is bearing, upside down, a plaster statuette of Mae West, the sort of prize won at shooting-galleries and carnival games of chance.*

BLANCHE [*stopping lifelessly at the steps*]: Well——

    MITCH *laughs uneasily.*

Well ...
MITCH: I guess it must be pretty late—and you're tired.
BLANCHE: Even the hot tamale man has deserted the street, and he hangs on till the end. [MITCH *laughs uneasily again.*] How will you get home?
MITCH: I'll walk over to Bourbon and catch an owl-car.
BLANCHE [*laughing grimly*]: Is that street-car named Desire still grinding along the tracks at this hour?
MITCH [*heavily*]: I'm afraid you haven't gotten much fun out of this evening, Blanche.
BLANCHE: I spoiled it for *you.*
MITCH: No, you didn't, but I felt all the time that I wasn't giving you much—entertainment.
BLANCHE: I simply couldn't rise to the occasion. That was all. I don't think I've ever tried so hard to be gay and made such a dismal mess of it. I get ten points for trying!—I *did* try.
MITCH: Why did you try if you didn't feel like it, Blanche?
BLANCHE: I was just obeying the law of nature.
MITCH: Which law is that?
BLANCHE: The one that says the lady must entertain the gentle-man—or no dice! See if you can locate my door-key in this purse. When I'm so tired my fingers are all thumbs!
MITCH [*rooting in her purse*]: This it?
BLANCHE: No, honey, that's the key to my trunk which I must soon be packing.

MITCH: You mean you are leaving here soon?
BLANCHE: I've outstayed my welcome.
MITCH: This it?

   The music fades away.

BLANCHE: Eureka! Honey, you open the door while I take a last
   look at the sky. [*She leans on the porch rail. He opens the door and
   stands awkwardly behind her.*] I'm looking for the Pleiades, the Seven
   Sisters, but these girls are not out tonight. Oh, yes they are, there
   they are! God bless them! All in a bunch going home from their
   little bridge party. . . . Y' get the door open? Good boy! I guess you
   —want to go now . . .

   He shuffles and coughs a little.

MITCH: Can I—uh—kiss you—good night?
BLANCHE: Why do you always ask me if you may?
MITCH: I don't know whether you want me to or not.
BLANCHE: Why should you be so doubtful?
MITCH: That night when we parked by the lake and I kissed you,
   you——
BLANCHE: Honey, it wasn't the kiss I objected to. I liked the kiss
   very much. It was the other little—familiarity—that I—felt obliged
   to—discourage. . . . I didn't resent it! Not a bit in the world!
   In fact, I was somewhat flattered that you—desired me! But,
   honey, you know as well as I do that a single girl, a girl alone
   in the world, has got to keep a firm hold on her emotions or she'll
   be lost!
MITCH [*solemnly*]: Lost?
BLANCHE: I guess you are used to girls that like to be lost. The
   kind that get lost immediately, on the first date!
MITCH: I like you to be exactly the way that you are, because in
   all my—experience—I have never known anyone like you.

   BLANCHE *looks at him gravely; then she bursts into laughter and
   then claps a hand to her mouth.*

MITCH: Are you laughing at me?
BLANCHE: No, honey. The lord and lady of the house have not
   yet returned, so come in. We'll have a night-cap. Let's leave the
   lights off. Shall we?
MITCH: You just—do what you want to.

BLANCHE *precedes him into the kitchen. The outer wall of the building disappears and the interiors of the two rooms can be dimly seen.*

BLANCHE [*remaining in the first room*]: The other room's more comfortable—go on in. This crashing around in the dark is my search for some liquor.

MITCH: You want a drink?

BLANCHE: I want *you* to have a drink! You have been so anxious and solemn all evening, and so have I; we have both been anxious and solemn and now for these few last remaining moments of our lives together—I want to create—*joie de vivre*! I'm lighting a candle.

MITCH: That's good.

BLANCHE: We are going to be very Bohemian. We are going to pretend that we are sitting in a little artists' cafe on the Left Bank in Paris! [*She lights a candle stub and puts it in a bottle.*] *Je suis la Dame aux Camellias! Vous êtes—Armand!* Understand French?

MITCH [*heavily*]: Naw. Naw, I——

BLANCHE: *Voulez-vous couchez avec moi ce soir? Vous ne comprenez pas? Ah, quel dommage!*—I mean it's a damned good thing. . . . I've found some liquor! Just enough for two shots without any dividends, honey . . .

MITCH [*heavily*]: That's—good.

She enters the bedroom with the drinks and the candle.

BLANCHE: Sit down! Why don't you take off your coat and loosen your collar?

MITCH: I better leave it on.

BLANCHE: No. I want you to be comfortable.

MITCH: I am ashamed of the way I perspire. My shirt is sticking to me.

BLANCHE: Perspiration is healthy. If people didn't perspire they would die in five minutes. [*She takes his coat from him.*] This is a nice coat. What kind of material is it?

MITCH: They call that stuff alpaca.

BLANCHE: Oh. Alpaca.

MITCH: It's very light weight alpaca.

BLANCHE: Oh. Light weight alpaca.

MITCH: I don't like to wear a wash-coat even in summer because I sweat through it.

BLANCHE: Oh.

MITCH: And it don't look neat on me. A man with a heavy build has got to be careful of what he puts on him so he don't look too clumsy.

BLANCHE: You are not too heavy.

MITCH: You don't think I am?

BLANCHE: You are not the delicate type. You have a massive bone-structure and a very imposing physique.

MITCH: Thank you. Last Christmas I was given a membership to the New Orleans Athletic Club.

BLANCHE: Oh, good.

MITCH: It was the finest present I ever was given. I work out there with the weights and I swim and I keep myself fit. When I started there, I was getting soft in the belly but now my belly is hard. It is so hard that now a man can punch me in the belly and it don't hurt me. Punch me! Go on! See? [*She pokes lightly at him.*]

BLANCHE: Gracious. [*Her hand touches her chest.*]

MITCH: Guess how much I weigh, Blanche?

BLANCHE: Oh, I'd say in the vicinity of—one hundred and eighty?

MITCH: Guess again.

BLANCHE: Not that much?

MITCH: No. More.

BLANCHE: Well, you're a tall man and you can carry a good deal of weight without looking awkward.

MITCH: I weigh two hundred and seven pounds and I'm six feet one and one half inches tall in my bare feet—without shoes on. And that is what I weigh stripped.

BLANCHE: Oh, my goodness, me! It's awe-inspiring.

MITCH [*embarrassed*]: My weight is not a very interesting subject to talk about. [*He hesitates for a moment.*] What's yours?

BLANCHE: My weight?

MITCH: Yes.

BLANCHE: Guess!

MITCH: Let me lift you.

BLANCHE: Samson! Go on, lift me. [*He comes behind her and puts his hand on her waist and raises her lightly off the ground.*] Well?

MITCH: You are light as a feather.

BLANCHE: Ha-ha! [*He lowers her but keeps his hands on her waist. BLANCHE speaks with an affectation of demureness.*] You may release me now.

MITCH: Huh?

BLANCHE [*gaily*]: I said unhand me, sir. [*He fumblingly embraces her. Her voice sounds gently reproving.*] Now, Mitch. Just because Stanley and Stella aren't at home is no reason why you shouldn't behave like a gentleman.

MITCH: Just give me a slap whenever I step out of bounds.

BLANCHE: That won't be necessary. You're a natural gentleman, one of the very few that are left in the world. I don't want you to think that I am severe and old maid school-teacherish or anything like that. It's just—well——

MITCH: Huh?

BLANCHE: I guess it is just that I have—old-fashioned ideals! [*She rolls her eyes, knowing he cannot see her face.* MITCH *goes to the front door. There is a considerable silence between them.* BLANCHE *sighs and* MITCH *coughs self-consciously.*]

MITCH [*finally*]: Where's Stanley and Stella tonight?

BLANCHE: They have gone out. With Mr. and Mrs. Hubbel upstairs.

MITCH: Where did they go?

BLANCHE: I think they were planning to go to a midnight prevue at Loew's State.

MITCH: We should all go out together some night.

BLANCHE: No. That wouldn't be a good plan.

MITCH: Why not?

BLANCHE: You are an old friend of Stanley's?

MITCH: We was together in the Two-forty-first.

BLANCHE: I guess he talks to you frankly?

MITCH: Sure.

BLANCHE: Has he talked to you about me?

MITCH: Oh—not very much.

BLANCHE: The way you say that, I suspect that he has.

MITCH: No, he hasn't said much.

BLANCHE: But what he *has* said. What would you say his attitude toward me was?

MITCH: Why do you want to ask that?

BLANCHE: Well——

MITCH: Don't you get along with him?

BLANCHE: What do you think?

MITCH: I don't think he understands you.

BLANCHE: That is putting it mildly. If it weren't for Stella about to have a baby, I wouldn't be able to endure things here.

MITCH: He isn't—nice to you?

BLANCHE: He is insufferably rude. Goes out of his way to offend me.

MITCH: In what way, Blanche?

BLANCHE: Why, in every conceivable way.

MITCH: I'm surprised to hear that.

BLANCHE: Are you?

MITCH: Well, I—don't see how anybody could be rude to you.

BLANCHE: It's really a pretty frightful situation. You see, there's no privacy here. There's just these portières between the two rooms at night. He stalks through the rooms in his underwear at night. And I have to ask him to close the bathroom door. That sort of commonness isn't necessary. You probably wonder why I don't move out. Well, I'll tell you frankly. A teacher's salary is barely sufficient for her living-expenses. I didn't save a penny last year and so I had to come here for the summer. That's why I have to put up with my sister's husband. And he has to put up with me, apparently so much against his wishes. . . . Surely he must have told you how much he hates me!

MITCH: I don't think he hates you.

BLANCHE: He hates me. Or why would he insult me? Of course there is such a thing as the hostility of—perhaps in some perverse kind of way he—No! To think of it makes me . . . [*She makes a gesture of revulsion. Then she finishes her drink. A pause follows.*]

MITCH: Blanche——

BLANCHE: Yes, honey?

MITCH: Can I ask you a question?

BLANCHE: Yes. What?

MITCH: How old are you?

She makes a nervous gesture.

BLANCHE: Why do you want to know?

MITCH: I talked to my mother about you and she said, "How old is Blanche?" And I wasn't able to tell her. [*There is another pause.*]

BLANCHE: You talked to your mother about me?

MITCH: Yes.

BLANCHE: Why?

MITCH: I told my mother how nice you were, and I liked you.

BLANCHE: Were you sincere about that?

MITCH: You know I was.

BLANCHE: Why did your mother want to know my age?

MITCH: Mother is sick.

BLANCHE: I'm sorry to hear it. Badly?

MITCH: She won't live long. Maybe just a few months.

BLANCHE: Oh.

MITCH: She worries because I'm not settled.

BLANCHE: Oh.

MITCH: She wants me to be settled down before she——— [*His voice is hoarse and he clears his throat twice, shuffling nervously around with his hands in and out of his pockets.*]

BLANCHE: You love her very much, don't you?

MITCH: Yes.

BLANCHE: I think you have a great capacity for devotion. You will be lonely when she passes on, won't you? [MITCH *clears his throat and nods.*] I understand what that is.

MITCH: To be lonely?

BLANCHE: I loved someone, too, and the person I loved I lost.

MITCH: Dead? [*She crosses to the window and sits on the sill, looking out. She pours herself another drink.*] A man?

BLANCHE: He was a boy, just a boy, when I was a very young girl. When I was sixteen, I made the discovery—love. All at once and much, much too completely. It was like you suddenly turned a blinding light on something that had always been half in shadow, that's how it struck the world for me. But I was unlucky. Deluded. There was something different about the boy, a nervousness, a softness and tenderness which wasn't like a man's, although he wasn't the least bit effeminate looking—still—that thing was there. . . . He came to me for help. I didn't know that. I didn't find out anything till after our marriage when we'd run away and come back and all I knew was I'd failed him in some mysterious way and wasn't able to give the help he needed but couldn't speak of! He was in the quicksands and clutching at me—but I wasn't holding him out, I was slipping in with him! I didn't know that. I didn't know anything except I loved him unendurably but without being able to help him or help myself. Then I found out. In the worst of all possible ways. By coming suddenly into a room that I thought was empty—which wasn't empty, but had two people in it . . .

A locomotive is heard approaching outside. She claps her hands to her ears and crouches over. The headlight of the locomotive glares into the room as it thunders past. As the noise recedes she straightens slowly and continues speaking.

Afterwards we pretended that nothing had been discovered. Yes, the three of us drove out to Moon Lake Casino, very drunk and laughing all the way.

Polka music sounds, in a minor key faint with distance.

We danced the Varsouviana! Suddenly in the middle of the dance the boy I had married broke away from me and ran out of the casino. A few moments later—a shot!

The Polka stops abruptly.
BLANCHE *rises stiffly. Then the Polka resumes in a major key.*

I ran out—all did!—all ran and gathered about the terrible thing at the edge of the lake! I couldn't get near for the crowding. Then somebody caught my arm. "Don't go any closer! Come back! You don't want to see!" See? See what! Then I heard voices say—Allan! Allan! The Grey boy! He'd stuck the revolver into his mouth, and fired—so that the back of his head had been—blown away!

She sways and covers her face.

It was because—on the dance-floor—unable to stop myself—I'd suddenly said—"I know! I know! You disgust me . . ." And then the searchlight which had been turned on the world was turned off again and never for one moment since has there been any light that's stronger than this—kitchen—candle. . . .

MITCH *gets up awkwardly and moves towards her a little. The Polka music increases.* MITCH *stands beside her.*

MITCH [*drawing her slowly into his arms*]: You need somebody. And I need somebody, too. Could it be—you and me, Blanche?

She stares at him vacantly for a moment. Then with a soft cry huddles in his embrace. She makes a sobbing effort to speak but the words won't come. He kisses her forehead and her eyes and finally her lips. The Polka tune fades out. Her breath is drawn and released in long, grateful sobs.

BLANCHE: Sometimes—there's God—so quickly!

SCENE VII

It is late afternoon in mid-September.
The portières are open and a table is set for a birthday supper, with cake and flowers.

STELLA *is completing the decorations as* STANLEY *comes in.*

STANLEY: What's all this stuff for?

STELLA: Honey, it's Blanche's birthday.

STANLEY: She here?

STELLA: In the bathroom.

STANLEY [*mimicking*]: "Washing out some things"?

STELLA: I reckon so.

STANLEY: How long she been in there?

STELLA: All afternoon.

STANLEY [*mimicking*]: "Soaking in a hot tub"?

STELLA: Yes.

STANLEY: Temperature 100 on the nose, and she soaks herself in a hot tub.

STELLA: She says it cools her off for the evening.

STANLEY: And you run out an' get her cokes, I suppose? And serve 'em to Her Majesty in the tub? [STELLA *shrugs*.] Set down here a minute.

STELLA: Stanley, I've got things to do.

STANLEY: Set down! I've got th' dope on your big sister, Stella.

STELLA: Stanley, stop picking on Blanche.

STANLEY: That girl calls *me* common!

STELLA: Lately you been doing all you can think of to rub her the wrong way, Stanley, and Blanche is sensitive and you've got to realize that Blanche and I grew up under very different circumstances than you did.

STANLEY: So I been told. And told and told and told! You know she's been feeding us a pack of lies here?

STELLA: No, I don't, and——

STANLEY: Well, she has, however. But now the cat's out of the bag! I found out some things!

STELLA: What—things?

STANLEY: Things I already suspected. But now I got proof from the most reliable sources—which I have checked on!

BLANCHE *is singing in the bathroom a saccharine popular ballad which is used contrapunctally with* STANLEY'S *speech.*

STELLA [*to* STANLEY]: Lower your voice!

STANLEY: Some canary-bird, huh!

STELLA: Now please tell me quietly what you think you've found out about my sister.

STANLEY: Lie Number One: All this squeamishness she puts on! You should just know the line she's been feeding to Mitch. He thought she had never been more than kissed by a fellow! But Sister Blanche is no lily! Ha-ha! Some lily she is!

STELLA: What have you heard and who from?

STANLEY: Our supply-man down at the plant has been going through Laurel for years and he knows all about her and everybody else in the town of Laurel knows all about her. She is as famous in Laurel as if she was the President of the United States, only she is not respected by any party! This supply-man stops at a hotel called the Flamingo.

BLANCHE [*singing blithely*]:
    "Say, it's only a paper moon, Sailing over a cardboard sea
        —But it wouldn't be make-believe If you believed in me!"

STELLA: What about the—Flamingo?

STANLEY: She stayed there, too.

STELLA: My sister lived at Belle Reve.

STANLEY: This is after the home-place had slipped through her lily-white fingers! She moved to the Flamingo! A second-class hotel which has the advantage of not interfering in the private social life of the personalities there! The Flamingo is used to all kinds of goings-on. But even the management of the Flamingo was impressed by Dame Blanche! In fact they were so impressed by Dame Blanche that they requested her to turn in her room-key —for permanently! This happened a couple of weeks before she showed here.

BLANCHE [*singing*]:
    "It's a Barnum and Bailey world, Just as phony as it can be—
        But it wouldn't be make-believe If you believed in me!"

STELLA: What—contemptible—lies!

STANLEY: Sure, I can see how you would be upset by this. She pulled the wool over your eyes as much as Mitch's!

STELLA: It's pure invention! There's not a word of truth in it and if I were a man and this creature had dared to invent such things in my presence——

BLANCHE [*singing*]:

> "Without your love,
> It's a honky-tonk parade!
> Without your love,
> It's a melody played In a penny arcade . . ."

STANLEY: Honey, I told you I thoroughly checked on these stories! Now wait till I finished. The trouble with Dame Blanche was that she couldn't put on her act any more in Laurel! They got wised up after two or three dates with her and then they quit, and she goes on to another, the same old lines, same old act, some old hooey! But the town was too small for this to go on forever! And as time went by she became a town character. Regarded as not just different but downright loco—nuts.

STELLA *draws back.*

And for the last year or two she has been washed up like poison. That's why she's here this summer, visiting royalty, putting on all this act—because she's practically told by the mayor to get out of town! Yes, did you know there was an army camp near Laurel and your sister's was one of the places called "Out-of-Bounds"?

BLANCHE:

> "It's only a paper moon, Just as phony as it can be—
> But it wouldn't be make-believe If you believed in me!"

STANLEY: Well, so much for her being such a refined and particular type of girl. Which brings us to Lie Number Two.

STELLA: I don't want to hear any more!

STANLEY: She's not going back to teach school! In fact I am willing to bet you that she never had no idea of returning to Laurel! She didn't resign temporarily from the high school because of her nerves! No, siree, Bob! She didn't. They kicked her out of that high school before the spring term ended—and I hate to tell you the reason that step was taken! A seventeen-year-old boy—she'd gotten mixed up with!

BLANCHE:

> "It's a Barnum and Bailey world, Just as phony as it can be——"

In the bathroom the water goes on loud; little breathless cries and peals of laughter are heard as if a child were frolicking in the tub.

STELLA: This is making me—sick!

STANLEY: The boy's dad learned about it and got in touch with the high school superintendent. Boy, oh, boy, I'd like to have been in that office when Dame Blanche was called on the carpet! I'd like to have seen her trying to squirm out of that one! But they had her on the hook good and proper that time and she knew that the jig was all up! They told her she better move on to some fresh territory. Yep, it was practickly a town ordinance passed against her!

The bathroom door is opened and BLANCHE *thrusts her head out holding a towel about her hair.*

BLANCHE: Stella!

STELLA [*faintly*]: Yes, Blanche?

BLANCHE: Give me another bath-towel to dry my hair with. I've just washed it.

STELLA: Yes, Blanche. [*She crosses in a dazed way from the kitchen to the bathroom door with a towel.*]

BLANCHE: What's the matter, honey?

STELLA: Matter? Why?

BLANCHE: You have such a strange expression on your face!

STELLA: Oh—— [*She tries to laugh.*] I guess I'm a little tired!

BLANCHE: Why don't you bathe, too, soon as I get out?

STANLEY [*calling from the kitchen*]: How soon is that going to be?

BLANCHE: Not so terribly long! Possess your soul in patience!

STANLEY: It's not my soul I'm worried about!

BLANCHE *slams the door.* STANLEY *laughs harshly.* STELLA *comes slowly back into the kitchen.*

STANLEY: Well, what do you think of it?

STELLA: I don't believe all of those stories and I think your supply-man was mean and rotten to tell them. It's possible that some of the things he said are partly true. There are things about my sister I don't approve of—things that caused sorrow at home. She was always—flighty!

STANLEY: Flighty is some word for it!

STELLA: But when she was young, very young, she had an experience that—killed her illusions!

STANLEY: What experience was that?

STELLA: I mean her marriage, when she was—almost a child! She married a boy who wrote poetry. . . . He was extremely good-looking. I think Blanche didn't just love him but worshipped the ground he walked on! Adored him and thought him almost too fine to be human! But then she found out——

STANLEY: What?

STELLA: This beautiful and talented young man was a degenerate. Didn't your supply-man give you that information?

STANLEY: All we discussed was recent history. That must have been a pretty long time ago.

STELLA: Yes, it was—a pretty long time ago. . . .

> STANLEY *comes up and takes her by the shoulders rather gently. She gently withdraws from him. Automatically she starts sticking little pink candles in the birthday cake.*

STANLEY: How many candles you putting in that cake?

STELLA: I'll stop at twenty-five.

STANLEY: Is company expected?

STELLA: We asked Mitch to come over for cake and ice-cream.

> STANLEY *looks a little uncomfortable. He lights a cigarette from the one he has just finished.*

STANLEY: I wouldn't be expecting Mitch over tonight.

> STELLA *pauses in her occupation with candles and looks slowly around at* STANLEY.

STELLA: *Why?*

STANLEY: Mitch is a buddy of mine. We were in the same outfit together—Two-forty-first Engineers. We work in the same plant and now on the same bowling team. You think I could face him if——

STELLA: Stanley Kowalski, did you—did you repeat what that——?

STANLEY: You're goddam right I told him! I'd have that on my conscience the rest of my life if I knew all that stuff and let my best friend get caught!

STELLA: Is Mitch through with her?

STANLEY: Wouldn't you be if——?

STELLA: I said, *Is Mitch through with her?*

> BLANCHE'S *voice is lifted again, serenely as a bell. She sings*
> *"But it wouldn't be make-believe If you believed in me."*

STANLEY: No, I don't think he's necessarily through with her—just wised up!

STELLA: Stanley, she thought Mitch was—going to—going to marry her. I was hoping so, too.

STANLEY: Well, he's not going to marry her. Maybe he *was*, but he's not going to jump in a tank with a school of sharks—now! [*He rises.*] Blanche! Oh, Blanche! Can I please get in my bathroom? [*There is a pause.*]

BLANCHE: Yes, indeed, sir! Can you wait one second while I dry?

STANLEY: Having waited one hour I guess one second ought to pass in a hurry.

STELLA: And she hasn't got her job? Well, what will she do!

STANLEY: She's not stayin' here after Tuesday. You know that, don't you? Just to make sure I bought her ticket myself. A bus-ticket!

STELLA: In the first place, Blanche wouldn't go on a bus.

STANLEY: She'll go on a bus and like it.

STELLA: No, she won't, no, she won't, Stanley!

STANLEY: *She'll go!* Period. P.S. She'll go *Tuesday!*

STELLA [*slowly*]: What'll—she—do? What on earth will she—do!

STANLEY: Her future is mapped out for her.

STELLA: What do you mean?

BLANCHE *sings.*

STANLEY: Hey, canary bird! Toots! Get *OUT* of the *BATHROOM!* Must I speak more plainly?

The bathroom door flies open and BLANCHE *emerges with a gay peal of laughter, but as* STANLEY *crosses past her, a frightened look appears in her face, almost a look of panic. He doesn't look at her but slams the bathroom door shut as he goes in.*

BLANCHE [*snatching up a hair-brush*]: Oh, I feel so good after my long, hot bath, I feel so good and cool and—rested!

STELLA [*sadly and doubtfully from the kitchen*]: Do you, Blanche?

BLANCHE [*brushing her hair vigorously*]: Yes, I do, so refreshed. [*She tinkles her highball glass.*] A hot bath and a long, cold drink always gives me a brand new outlook on life! [*She looks through the portières at* STELLA, *standing between them, and slowly stops brushing.*] Something has happened!—What is it?

STELLA [*turning quickly away*]: Why, nothing has happened, Blanche.

BLANCHE: You're lying! Something has!

She stares fearfully at STELLA, *who pretends to be busy at the table. The distant piano goes into a hectic breakdown.*

SCENE VIII

Three-quarters of an hour later.
The view through the big windows is fading gradually into a still-golden dusk. A torch of sunlight blazes on the side of a big water-tank or oil-drum across the empty lot toward the business district which is now pierced by pin-points of lighted windows or windows reflecting the sunset.

> *The three people are completing a dismal birthday supper. STANLEY looks sullen. STELLA is embarrassed and sad.*
>
> *BLANCHE has a tight, artificial smile on her drawn face. There is a fourth place at the table which is left vacant.*

BLANCHE [*suddenly*]: Stanley, tell us a joke, tell us a funny story to make us all laugh. I don't know what's the matter, we're all so solemn. Is it because I've been stood up by my beau?

> STELLA *laughs feebly.*

It's the first time in my entire experience with men, and I've had a good deal of all sorts, that I've actually been stood up by anybody! Ha-ha! I don't know how to take it. . . . Tell us a funny little story, Stanley! Something to help us out.
STANLEY: I didn't think you liked my stories, Blanche.
BLANCHE: I like them when they're amusing but not indecent.
STANLEY: I don't know any refined enough for your taste.
BLANCHE: Then let me tell one.
STELLA: Yes, you tell one, Blanche. You used to know lots of good stories.

> *The music fades.*

BLANCHE: Let me see, now. . . . I must run through my repertoire! Oh, yes—I love parrot stories! Do you all like parrot stories? Well, this one's about the old maid and the parrot. This old maid, she had a parrot that cursed a blue streak and knew more vulgar expressions than Mr. Kowalski!
STANLEY: Huh.
BLANCHE: And the only way to hush the parrot up was to put the cover back on its cage so it would think it was night and go back to sleep. Well, one morning the old maid had just uncovered the

parrot for the day—when who should she see coming up the front walk but the preacher! Well, she rushed back to the parrot and slipped the cover back on the cage and then she let in the preacher. And the parrot was perfectly still, just as quiet as a mouse, but just as she was asking the preacher how much sugar he wanted in his coffee—the parrot broke the silence with a loud—(*she whistles*) —and said—"God *damn*, but that was a short day!"

> *She throws back her head and laughs.* STELLA *also makes an ineffectual effort to seem amused.* STANLEY *pays no attention to the story but reaches way over the table to spear his fork into the remaining chop which he eats with his fingers.*

BLANCHE: Apparently Mr. Kowalski was not amused.

STELLA: Mr. Kowalski is too busy making a pig of himself to think of anything else!

STANLEY: That's right, baby.

STELLA: Your face and your fingers are disgustingly greasy. Go and wash up and then help me clear the table.

> *He hurls a plate to the floor.*

STANLEY: That's how I'll clear the table! [*He seizes her arm.*] Don't ever talk that way to me! "Pig—Polack—disgusting—vulgar—greasy!"—them kind of words have been on your tongue and your sister's too much around here! What do you two think you are? A pair of queens? Remember what Huey Long said—"Every Man is a King!" And I am the king around here, so don't forget it! [*He hurls a cup and saucer to the floor.*] My place is cleared! You want me to clear your places?

> STELLA *begins to cry weakly.* STANLEY *stalks out on the porch and lights a cigarette.*
> *The Negro entertainers around the corner are heard.*

BLANCHE: What happened while I was bathing? What did he tell you, Stella?

STELLA: Nothing, nothing, nothing!

BLANCHE: I think he told you something about Mitch and me! You know why Mitch didn't come but you won't tell me! [STELLA *shakes her head helplessly.*] I'm going to call him!

STELLA: I wouldn't call him, Blanche.

BLANCHE: I am, I'm going to call him on the phone.

STELLA [*miserably*]: I wish you wouldn't.

BLANCHE: I intend to be given some explanation from someone!

> *She rushes to the phone in the bedroom.* STELLA *goes out on the porch and stares reproachfully at her husband. He grunts and turns away from her.*

STELLA: I hope you're pleased with your doings. I never had so much trouble swallowing food in my life, looking at the girl's face and the empty chair. [*She cries quietly.*]

BLANCHE [*at the phone*]: Hello. Mr. Mitchell, please. . . . Oh. . . . I would like to leave a number if I may. Magnolia 9047. And say it's important to call. . . . Yes, very important. . . . Thank you. [*She remains by the phone with a lost, frightened look.*]

> STANLEY *turns slowly back towards his wife and takes her clumsily in his arms.*

STANLEY: Stell, it's gonna be all right after she goes and after you've had the baby. It's gonna be all right again between you and me the way that it was. You remember that way that it was? Them nights we had together? God, honey, it's gonna be sweet when we can make noise in the night the way that we used to and get the coloured lights going with nobody's sister behind the curtains to hear us!

> *Their upstairs neighbours are heard in bellowing laughter at something.* STANLEY *chuckles.*

Steve an' Eunice . . .

STELLA: Come on back in. [*She returns to the kitchen and starts lighting the candles on the white cake.*] Blanche?

BLANCHE: Yes. [*She returns from the bedroom to the table in the kitchen.*] Oh, those pretty, pretty little candles! Oh, don't burn them, Stella.

STELLA: I certainly will.

> STANLEY *comes back in.*

BLANCHE: You ought to save them for baby's birthdays. Oh, I hope candles are going to glow in his life and I hope that his eyes are going to be like candles, like two blue candles lighted in a white cake!

STANLEY [*sitting down*]: What poetry!

BLANCHE: His Auntie knows candles aren't safe, that candles burn out in little boys' and girls' eyes, or wind blows them out and after that happens, electric light bulbs go on and you see too plainly . . . [*She pauses reflectively for a moment.*] I shouldn't have called him.

STELLA: There's lots of things could have happened.

BLANCHE: There's no excuse for it, Stella. I don't have to put up with insults. I won't be taken for granted.

STANLEY: Goddamn, it's hot in here with the steam from the bathroom.

BLANCHE: I've said I was sorry three times. [*The piano fades out.*] I take hot baths for my nerves. Hydro-therapy, they call it. You healthy Polack, without a nerve in your body, of course you don't know what anxiety feels like!

STANLEY: I am not a Polack. People from Poland are Poles, not Polacks. But what I am is a one hundred per cent. American, born and raised in the greatest country on earth and proud as hell of it, so don't ever call me a Polack.

The phone rings. BLANCHE rises expectantly.

BLANCHE: Oh, that's for me, I'm sure.

STANLEY: *I'm* not sure. Keep your seat. [*He crosses leisurely to phone.*] H'lo. Aw, yeh, hello, Mac.

He leans against wall, staring insultingly in at BLANCHE. She sinks back in her chair with a frightened look. STELLA leans over and touches her shoulder.

BLANCHE: Oh, keep your hands off me, Stella. What is the matter with you? Why do you look at me with that pitying look?

STANLEY [*bawling*]: QUIET IN THERE!—We've got a noisy woman on the place.—Go on, Mac. At Riley's? No, I don't wanta bowl at Riley's. I had a little trouble with Riley last week. I'm the team-captain, ain't I? All right, then, we're not gonna bowl at Riley's, we're gonna bowl at the West Side or the Gala! All right, Mac. See you!

He hangs up and returns to the table. BLANCHE fiercely controls herself, drinking quietly from her tumbler of water. He doesn't look at her but reaches in a pocket. Then he speaks slowly and with false amiability.

Sister Blanche, I've got a little birthday remembrance for you.

BLANCHE: Oh, have you, Stanley? I wasn't expecting any, I—I don't know why Stella wants to observe my birthday! I'd much rather forget it—when you—reach twenty-seven! Well—age is a subject that you'd prefer to—ignore!

STANLEY: Twenty-seven?

BLANCHE [*quickly*]: What is it? Is it for *me*?

He is holding a little envelope towards her.

STANLEY: Yes, I hope you like it!

BLANCHE: Why, why—— Why, it's a——

STANLEY: Ticket! Back to Laurel! On the Greyhound! Tuesday!

The Varsouviana music steals in softly and continues playing. STELLA *rises abruptly and turns her back.* BLANCHE *tries to smile. Then she tries to laugh. Then she gives both up and springs from the table and runs into the next room. She clutches her throat and then runs into the bathroom. Coughing, gagging sounds are heard.*

Well!

STELLA: You didn't need to do that.

STANLEY: Don't forget all that I took off her.

STELLA: You needn't have been so cruel to someone alone as she is.

STANLEY: Delicate piece she is.

STELLA: She is. She was. You didn't know Blanche as a girl. Nobody, nobody, was tender and trusting as she was. But people like you abused her, and forced her to change.

He crosses into the bedroom, ripping off his shirt, and changes into a brilliant silk bowling shirt. She follows him.

Do you think you're going bowling now?

STANLEY: Sure.

STELLA: You're not going bowling. [*She catches hold of his shirt.*] Why did you do this to her?

STANLEY: I done nothing to no one. Let go of my shirt. You've torn it.

STELLA: I want to know why. Tell me why.

STANLEY: When we first met, me and you, you thought I was common. How right you was, baby. I was common as dirt. You showed me the snapshot of the place with the columns. I pulled you down off them columns and how you loved it, having them coloured lights going! And wasn't we happy together, wasn't it all okay till she showed here?

STELLA *makes a slight movement. Her look goes suddenly inward as if some interior voice had called her name. She begins a slow, shuffling progress from the bedroom to the kitchen, leaning and resting on the back of the chair and then on the edge of a table with a blind look and listening expression.* STANLEY, *finishing with his shirt, is unaware of her reaction.*

And wasn't we happy together? Wasn't it all okay? Till she showed here. Hoity-toity, describing me as an ape. [*He suddenly notices the change in* STELLA.] Hey, what is it, Stel? [*He crosses to her.*]
STELLA [*quietly*]: Take me to the hospital.

He is with her now, supporting her with his arm, murmuring indistinguishably as they go outside. The "Varsouviana" is heard, its music rising with sinister rapidity as the bathroom door opens slightly. BLANCHE *comes out twisting a washcloth. She begins to whisper the words as the light fades slowly.*

BLANCHE: *El pan de mais, el pan de mais,*
             El pan de mais sin sal.
             El pan de mais, el pan de mais,
             El pan de mais sin sal . . .

SCENE IX

A while later that evening. BLANCHE *is seated in a tense hunched position in a bedroom chair that she has re-covered with diagonal green and white stripes. She has on her scarlet satin robe. On the table beside chair is a bottle of liquor and a glass. The rapid, feverish polka tune, the "Varsouviana," is heard. The music is in her mind; she is drinking to escape it and the sense of disaster closing in on her, and she seems to whisper the words of the song. An electric fan is turning back and forth across her.*

MITCH *comes around the corner in work clothes: blue denim shirt and pants. He is unshaven. He climbs the steps to the door and rings.* BLANCHE *is startled*

BLANCHE: Who is it, please?
MITCH [*hoarsely*]: Me. Mitch.

The polka tune stops.

BLANCHE: Mitch!—Just a minute.

She rushes about frantically, hiding the bottle in a closet, crouching at the mirror and dabbing her face with cologne and powder. She is so excited that her breath is audible as she dashes about. At last she rushes to the door in the kitchen and lets him in.

Mitch!—Y'know, I really shouldn't let you in after the treatment I have received from you this evening! So utterly uncavalier! But hello, beautiful!

She offers him her lips. He ignores it and pushes past her into the flat. She looks fearfully after him as he stalks into the bedroom.

My, my, what a cold shoulder! And a face like a thundercloud! And such uncouth apparel! Why, you haven't even shaved! The unforgivable insult to a lady! But I forgive you. I forgive you because it's such a relief to see you. You've stopped that polka tune that I had caught in my head. Have you ever had anything caught in your head? Some words, a piece of music? That goes relentlessly on and on in your head? No, of course you haven't, you dumb angel-puss, you'd never get anything awful caught in your head!

He stares at her while she follows him while she talks. It is obvious that he has had a few drinks on the way over.

MITCH: Do we have to have that fan on?
BLANCHE: No!
MITCH: I don't like fans.
BLANCHE: Then let's turn it off, honey. I'm not partial to them!

She presses the switch and the fan nods slowly off. She clears her throat uneasily as MITCH *plumps himself down on the bed in the bedroom and lights a cigarette.*

I don't know what there is to drink. I—haven't investigated.
MITCH: I don't want Stan's liquor.
BLANCHE: It isn't Stan's. Everything here isn't Stan's. Some things on the premises are actually mine! How is your mother? Isn't your mother well?
MITCH: Why?
BLANCHE: Something's the matter tonight, but never mind. I won't cross-examine the witness. I'll just—— [*She touches her forehead vaguely. The polka tune starts up again.*]—pretend I don't notice anything different about you! That—music again . . .
MITCH: What music?

BLANCHE: The "Varsouviana"? The polka tune they were playing when Allan—— Wait!

A distant revolver shot is heard. BLANCHE *seems relieved.*

There now, the shot! It always stops after that.

The polka music dies out again.

Yes, now it's stopped.

MITCH: Are you boxed out of your mind?

BLANCHE: I'll go and see what I can find in the way of—— [*She crosses into the closet, pretending to search for the bottle.*] Oh, by the way, excuse me for not being dressed. But I'd practically given you up! Had you forgotten your invitation to supper?

MITCH: I wasn't going to see you any more.

BLANCHE: Wait a minute. I can't hear what you're saying and you talk so little that when you do say something, I don't want to miss a single syllable of it. . . . What am I looking around here for? Oh, yes—liquor! We've had so much excitement around here this evening that I *am* boxed out of my mind! [*She pretends suddenly to find the bottle. He draws his foot up on the bed and stares at her contemptuously.*] Here's something. Southern Comfort! What is that, I wonder?

MITCH: If you don't know, it must belong to Stan.

BLANCHE: Take your foot off the bed. It has a light cover on it. Of course you boys don't notice things like that. I've done so much with this place since I've been here.

MITCH: I bet you have.

BLANCHE: You saw it before I came. Well, look at it now! This room is almost—dainty! I want to keep it that way. I wonder if this stuff ought to be mixed with something? Ummm, it's sweet, so sweet! It's terribly, terribly sweet! Why, it's a *liqueur*, I believe! Yes, that's what it *is*, a liqueur! [MITCH *grunts.*] I'm afraid you won't like it, but try it, and maybe you will.

MITCH: I told you already I don't want none of his liquor and I mean it. You ought to lay off his liquor. He says you been lapping it up all summer like a wild-cat!

BLANCHE: What a fantastic statement! Fantastic of him to say it, fantastic of you to repeat it! I won't descend to the level of such cheap accusations to answer them, even!

MITCH: Huh.

BLANCHE: What's in your mind? I see something in your eyes!

MITCH [*getting up*]: It's dark in here.

BLANCHE: I like it dark. The dark is comforting to me.

MITCH: I don't think I ever seen you in the light. [BLANCHE *laughs breathlessly.*] That's a fact!

BLANCHE: Is it?

MITCH: I've never seen you in the afternoon.

BLANCHE: Whose fault is that?

MITCH: You never want to go out in the afternoon.

BLANCHE: Why, Mitch, you're at the plant in the afternoon!

MITCH: Not Sunday afternoon. I've asked you to go out with me sometimes on Sundays but you always make an excuse. You never want to go out till after six and then it's always some place that's not lighted much.

BLANCHE: There is some obscure meaning in this but I fail to catch it.

MITCH: What it means is I've never had a real good look at you, Blanche.

BLANCHE: What are you leading up to?

MITCH: Let's turn the light on here.

BLANCHE [*fearfully*]: Light? Which light? What for?

MITCH: This one with the paper thing on it. [*He tears the paper lantern off the light bulb. She utters a frightened gasp.*]

BLANCHE: What did you do that for?

MITCH: So I can take a look at you good and plain!

BLANCHE: Of course you don't really mean to be insulting!

MITCH: No, just realistic.

BLANCHE: I don't want realism.

MITCH: Naw, I guess not.

BLANCHE: I'll tell you what I want. Magic! [MITCH *laughs.*] Yes, yes, magic! I try to give that to people. I misrepresent things to them. I don't tell truth, I tell what *ought* to be truth. And if that is sinful, then let me be damned for it!—*Don't turn the light on!*

MITCH *crosses to the switch. He turns the light on and stares at her. She cries out and covers her face. He turns the light off again.*

MITCH [*slowly and bitterly*]: I don't mind you being older than what I thought. But all the rest of it—God! That pitch about your ideals being so old-fashioned and all the malarkey that you've dished out all summer. Oh, I knew you weren't sixteen any more. But I was a fool enough to believe you was straight.

BLANCHE: Who told you I wasn't—"straight"? My loving brother-in-law. And you believed him.

MITCH: I called him a liar at first. And then I checked on the story. First I asked our supply-man who travels through Laurel. And then I talked directly over long-distance to this merchant.

BLANCHE: Who is the merchant?

MITCH: Kiefaber.

BLANCHE: The merchant Kiefaber of Laurel! I know the man. He whistled at me. I put him in his place. So now for revenge he makes up stories about me.

MITCH: Three people, Kiefaber, Stanley and Shaw, swore to them!

BLANCHE: Rub-a-dub-dub, three men in a tub! And such a filthy tub!

MITCH: Didn't you stay at a hotel called The Flamingo?

BLANCHE: Flamingo? No! Tarantula was the name of it! I stayed at a hotel called The Tarantula Arms!

MITCH [*stupidly*]: Tarantula?

BLANCHE: Yes, a big spider! That's where I brought my victims. [*She pours herself another drink.*] Yes, I had many intimacies with strangers. After the death of Allan—intimacies with strangers was all I seemed able to fill my empty heart with. . . . I think it was panic, just panic, that drove me from one to another, hunting for some protection—here and there, in the most—unlikely places —even, at last, in a seventeen-year-old boy but—somebody wrote the superintendent about it—"This woman is morally unfit for her position!"

She throws back her head with convulsive, sobbing laughter.
Then she repeats the statement, gasps, and drinks.

True? Yes, I suppose—unfit somehow—anyway. . . . So I came here. There was nowhere else I could go. I was played out. You know what played out is? My youth was suddenly gone up the water-spout, and—I met you. You said you needed somebody. Well, I needed somebody, too. I thanked God for you, because you seemed to be gentle—a cleft in the rock of the world that I could hide in! The poor man's Paradise—is a little peace. . . . But I guess I was asking, hoping—too much! Kiefaber, Stanley and Shaw have tied an old tin can to the tail of the kite.

There is a pause. MITCH *stares at her dumbly.*

MITCH: You lied to me, Blanche.

BLANCHE: Don't say I lied to you.

MITCH: Lies, lies, inside and out, all lies.

BLANCHE: Never inside, I didn't lie in my heart. . . .

A Vendor comes around the corner. She is a blind MEXICAN WOMAN *in a dark shawl, carrying bunches of those gaudy tin flowers that lower class Mexicans display at funerals and other festive occasions. She is calling barely audibly. Her figure is only faintly visible outside the building.*

MEXICAN WOMAN: *Flores. Flores. Flores para los muertos. Flores. Flores.*

BLANCHE: What? Oh! Somebody outside. . . . I—I lived in a house where dying old women remembered their dead men . . .

MEXICAN WOMEN: *Flores. Flores para los muertos* . . .

The polka tune fades in.

BLANCHE [*as if to herself*]: Crumble and fade and—regrets—re-criminations . . . "If you'd done this, it wouldn't've cost me that!"

MEXICAN WOMAN: *Corones para los muertos. Corones* . . .

BLANCHE: Legacies! Huh. . . . And other things such as blood-stained pillow-slips—"Her linen needs changing"—"Yes Mother. But couldn't we get a coloured girl to do it?" No, we couldn't of course. Everything gone but the——

MEXICAN WOMAN: *Flores.*

BLANCHE: Death—I used to sit here and she used to sit over there and death was as close as you are. . . . We didn't dare even admit we had ever heard of it!

MEXICAN WOMAN: *Flores para los muertos, flores—flores* . . .

BLANCHE: The opposite is desire. So do you wonder? How could you possibly wonder! Not far from Belle Reve, before we had lost Belle Reve, was a camp where they trained young soldiers. On Saturday nights they would go in town to get drunk——

MEXICAN WOMAN [*softly*]: *Corones* . . .

BLANCHE: —and on the way back they would stagger on to my lawn and call—"Blanche! Blanche!"—The deaf old lady remaining suspected nothing. But sometimes I slipped outside to answer their calls. . . . Later the paddy-wagon would gather them up like daisies . . . the long way home . . .

The MEXICAN WOMAN *turns slowly and drifts back off with her soft mournful cries.* BLANCHE *goes to the dresser and leans forward on it. After a moment,* MITCH *rises and follows her purposefully. The polka music fades away. He places his hands on her waist and tries to turn her about.*

BLANCHE: What do you want?

MITCH [*fumbling to embrace her*]: What I been missing all summer.

BLANCHE: Then marry me, Mitch!

MITCH: I don't think I want to marry you any more.

BLANCHE: No?

MITCH [*dropping his hands from her waist*]: You're not clean enough to bring in the house with my mother.

BLANCHE: Go away, then. [*He stares at her.*] Get out of here quick before I start screaming fire! [*Her throat is tightening with hysteria.*] Get out of here quick before I start screaming fire.

He still remains staring. She suddenly rushes to the big window with its pale blue square of the soft summer light and cries wildly.

Fire! Fire! Fire!

With a startled gasp, MITCH turns and goes out of the outer door, clatters awkwardly down the steps and around the corner of the building. BLANCHE staggers back from the window and falls to her knees. The distant piano is slow and blue.

SCENE X

It is a few hours later that night.

BLANCHE *has been drinking fairly steadily since* MITCH *left. She has dragged her wardrobe trunk into the centre of the bedroom. It hangs open with flowery dresses thrown across it. As the drinking and packing went on, a mood of hysterical exhilaration came into her and she has decked herself out in a somewhat soiled and crumpled white satin evening gown and a pair of scuffed silver slippers with brilliants set in their heels.*

Now she is placing the rhinestone tiara on her head before the mirror of the dressing-table and murmuring excitedly as if to a group of spectral admirers.

BLANCHE: How about taking a swim, a moonlight swim at the old rock-quarry? If anyone's sober enough to drive a car! Ha-Ha! Best way in the world to stop your head buzzing! Only you've got to be careful to dive where the deep pool is—if you hit a rock you don't come up till tomorrow. . . .

Tremblingly she lifts the hand mirror for a closer inspection. She

*catches her breath and slams the mirror face down with such violence
that the glass cracks. She moans a little and attempts to rise.*

STANLEY *appears around the corner of the building. He still has on
the vivid green silk bowling shirt As he rounds the corner the honky-
tonk music is heard. It continues softly throughout the scene.*

He enters the kitchen, slamming the door. As he peers in at BLANCHE,
*he gives a low whistle. He has had a few drinks on the way and has
brought some quart beer bottles home with him.*

BLANCHE: How is my sister?

STANLEY: She is doing okay.

BLANCHE: And how is the baby?

STANLEY [*grinning amiably*]: The baby won't come before morning
so they told me to go home and get a little shut-eye.

BLANCHE: Does that mean we are to be alone in here?

STANLEY: Yep. Just me and you, Blanche. Unless you got somebody
hid under the bed. What've you got on those fine feathers for?

BLANCHE: Oh, that's right. You left before my wire came.

STANLEY: You got a wire?

BLANCHE: I received a telegram from an old admirer of mine.

STANLEY: Anything good?

BLANCHE: I think so. An invitation.

STANLEY: What to? A fireman's ball?

BLANCHE [*throwing back her head*]: A cruise of the Caribbean on a
yacht!

STANLEY: Well, well. What do you know?

BLANCHE: I have never been so surprised in my life.

STANLEY: I guess not.

BLANCHE: It came like a bolt from the blue!

STANLEY: Who did you say it was from?

BLANCHE: An old beau of mine.

STANLEY: The one that give you the white fox-pieces?

BLANCHE: Mr. Shep Huntleigh. I wore his ATO pin my last year
at college. I hadn't seen him again until last Christmas. I ran in
to him on Biscayne Boulevard. Then—just now—this wire—
inviting me on a cruise of the Caribbean! The problem is clothes.
I tore into my trunk to see what I have that's suitable for the tropics!

STANLEY: And come up with that—gorgeous—diamond—tiara?

BLANCHE: This old relic! Ha-ha! It's only rhinestones.

STANLEY: Gosh. I thought it was Tiffany diamonds. [*He unbuttons
his shirt.*]

BLANCHE: Well, anyhow, I shall be entertained in style.

STANLEY: Uh-huh. It goes to show, you never know what is coming.

BLANCHE: Just when I thought my luck had begun to fail me——

STANLEY: Into the picture pops this Miami millionaire.

BLANCHE: This man is not from Miami. This man is from Dallas.

STANLEY: This man is from Dallas?

BLANCHE: Yes, this man is from Dallas where gold spouts out of the ground!

STANLEY: Well, just so he's from somewhere! [*He starts removing his shirt.*]

BLANCHE: Close the curtains before you undress any further.

STANLEY [*amiably*]: This is all I'm going to undress right now. [*He rips the sack off a quart beer-bottle.*] Seen a bottle-opener?

> *She moves slowly towards the dresser, where she stands with her hands knotted together.*

I used to have a cousin who could open a beer-bottle with his teeth. [*Pounding the bottle cap on the corner of table.*] That was his only accomplishment, all he could do—he was just a human bottle-opener. And then one time, at a wedding party, he broke his front teeth off! After that he was so ashamed of himself he used t' sneak out of the house when company came . . .

> *The bottle cap pops off and a geyser of foam shoots up.* STANLEY *laughs happily, holding up the bottle over his head.*

Ha-ha! Rain from heaven! [*He extends the bottle towards her.*] Shall we bury the hatchet and make it a loving-cup? Huh?

BLANCHE: No, thank you.

STANLEY: Well, it's a red letter night for us both. You having an oil-millionaire and me having a baby.

> *He goes to the bureau in the bedroom and crouches to remove something from the bottom drawer.*

BLANCHE [*drawing back*]: What are you doing in here?

STANLEY: Here's something I always break out on special occasions like this! The silk pyjamas I wore on my wedding night!

BLANCHE: Oh.

STANLEY: When the telephone rings and they say, "You've got a son!" I'll tear this off and wave it like a flag! [*He shakes out a brilliant pyjama coat.*] I guess we are both entitled to put on the dog. [*He goes back to the kitchen with the coat over his arm.*]

BLANCHE: When I think of how divine it is going to be to have such a thing as privacy once more—I could weep with joy!

STANLEY: This millionaire from Dallas is not going to interfere with your privacy any?

BLANCHE: It won't be the sort of thing you have in mind. This man is a gentleman and he respects me. [*Improvising feverishly.*] What he wants is my companionship. Having great wealth sometimes makes people lonely!

STANLEY: I wouldn't know about that.

BLANCHE: A cultivated woman, a woman of intelligence and breeding, can enrich a man's life—immeasurably! I have those things to offer, and this doesn't take them away. Physical beauty is passing. A transitory possession. But beauty of the mind and richness of the spirit and tenderness of the heart—and I have all of those things—aren't taken away, but grow! Increase with the years! How strange that I should be called a destitute woman! When I have all of these treasures locked in my heart. [*A choked sob comes from her.*] I think of myself as a very, very rich woman! But I have been foolish—casting my pearls before swine!

STANLEY: Swine, huh?

BLANCHE: Yes, swine! Swine! And I'm thinking not only of you but of your friend, Mr. Mitchell. He came to see me tonight. He dared to come here in his work-clothes! And to repeat slander to me, vicious stories that he had gotten from you! I gave him his walking papers . . .

STANLEY: You did, huh?

BLANCHE: But then he came back. He returned with a box of roses to beg my forgiveness! He implored my forgiveness. But some things are not forgivable. Deliberate cruelty is not forgivable. It is the one unforgivable thing in my opinion and it is the one thing of which I have never, never been guilty. And so I told him, I said to him, "Thank you," but it was foolish of me to think that we could ever adapt ourselves to each other. Our ways of life are too different. Our attitudes and our backgrounds are incompatible. We have to be realistic about such things. So farewell, my friend! And let there be no hard feelings . . .

STANLEY: Was this before or after the telegram came from the Texas oil millionaire?

BLANCHE: What telegram? No! No, after! As a matter of fact, the wire came just as——

STANLEY: As a matter of fact there wasn't no wire at all!

BLANCHE: Oh, oh!

STANLEY: There isn't no millionaire! And Mitch didn't come back with roses 'cause I know where he is——

BLANCHE: Oh!

STANLEY: There isn't a goddam thing but imagination!

BLANCHE: Oh!

STANLEY: And lies and conceit and tricks!

BLANCHE: Oh!

STANLEY: And look at yourself! Take a look at yourself in that worn-out Mardi Gras outfit, rented for fifty cents from some rag-picker! And with the crazy crown on! What queen do you think you are!

BLANCHE: Oh—God ...

STANLEY: I've been on to you from the start! Not once did you pull any wool over this boy's eyes! You come in here and sprinkle the place with powder and spray perfume and cover the light-bulb with a paper lantern, and lo and behold the place has turned into Egypt and you are the Queen of the Nile! Sitting on your throne and swilling down my liquor! I say—*Ha—Ha! Do you hear me? Ha—ha—ha!* [*He walks into the bedroom.*]

BLANCHE: Don't come in here!

Lurid reflections appear on the walls around BLANCHE. *The shadows are of a grotesque and menacing form. She catches her breath, crosses to the phone and jiggles the hook.* STANLEY *goes into the bathroom and closes the door.*

Operator, operator! Give me long-distance, please. . . . I want to get in touch with Mr. Shep Huntleigh of Dallas. He's so well-known he doesn't require any address. Just ask anybody who—— Wait!—No, I couldn't find it right now. . . . Please understand, I—No! No, wait! . . . One moment! Someone is—Nothing! Hold on, please!

She sets the phone down and crosses warily into the kitchen.
The night is filled with inhuman voices like cries in a jungle.
The shadows and lurid reflections move sinuously as flames along the wall spaces.
Through the back wall of the rooms, which have become transparent, can be seen the sidewalk. A prostitute has rolled a drunkard. He pursues her along the walk, overtakes her and there is a struggle. A policeman's whistle breaks it up. The figures disappear.

Some moments later the NEGRO WOMAN *appears around the corner with a sequined bag which the prostitute had dropped on the walk. She is rooting excitedly through it.*

BLANCHE *presses her knuckles to her lips and returns slowly to the phone. She speaks in a hoarse whisper.*

Operator! Operator! Never mind long-distance. Get Western Union. There isn't time to be—Western—Western Union!

She waits anxiously.

Western Union? Yes! I—want to—— Take down this message! "In desperate, desperate circumstances! Help me! Caught in a trap. Caught in——" Oh!

The bathroom door is thrown open and STANLEY *comes out in the brilliant silk pyjamas. He grins at her as he knots the tasselled sash about his waist. She gasps and backs away from the phone. He stares at her for a count of ten. Then a clicking becomes audible from the telephone, steady and rasping.*

STANLEY: You left th' phone off th' hook.

He crosses to it deliberately and sets it back on the hook. After he has replaced it, he stares at her again, his mouth slowly curving into a grin, as he waves between BLANCHE *and the outer door.*

The barely audible "blue piano" begins to drum up louder. The sound of it turns into the roar of an approaching locomotive. BLANCHE *crouches, pressing her fists to her ears until it has gone by.*

BLANCHE [*finally straightening*]: Let me—let me get by you!

STANLEY: Get by me? Sure. Go ahead. [*He moves back a pace in the doorway.*]

BLANCHE: You—you stand over there! [*She indicates a further position.*]

STANLEY [*grinning*]: You got plenty of room to walk by me now.

BLANCHE: Not with you there! But I've got to get out somehow!

STANLEY: You think I'll interfere with you? Ha-ha!

The "blue piano" goes softly. She turns confusedly and makes a faint gesture. The inhuman jungle voices rise up. He takes a step towards her, biting his tongue which protrudes between his lips.

STANLEY [*softly*]: Come to think of it—maybe you wouldn't be bad to—interfere with . . .

BLANCHE *moves backward through the door into the bedroom.*

BLANCHE: Stay back! Don't you come towards me another step or
    I'll——
STANLEY: What?
BLANCHE: Some awful thing will happen! It will!
STANLEY: What are you putting on now?

They are now both inside the bedroom.

BLANCHE: I warn you, don't, I'm in danger!

*He takes another step. She smashes a bottle on the table and faces
him, clutching the broken top.*

STANLEY: What did you do that for?
BLANCHE: So I could twist the broken end in your face!
STANLEY: I bet you would do that!
BLANCHE: I would! I will if you——
STANLEY: Oh! So you want some rough-house! All right, let's
    have some rough-house!

*He springs towards her, overturning the table. She cries out and strikes
at him with the bottle top but he catches her wrist.*

Tiger—tiger! Drop the bottle-top! Drop it! We've had this date with
    each other from the beginning!

*She moans. The bottle-top falls. She sinks to her knees. He picks
up her inert figure and carries her to the bed. The hot trumpet and
drums from the Four Deuces sound loudly.*

SCENE XI

*It is some weeks later. STELLA is packing BLANCHE'S things. Sound
of water can be heard running in the bathroom.
The portières are partly open on the poker players—STANLEY, STEVE,
MITCH and PABLO—who sit around the table in the kitchen. The atmosphere of the kitchen is now the same raw, lurid one of the disastrous poker
night.
The building is framed by the sky of turquoise. STELLA has been crying
as she arranges the flowery dresses in the open trunk.*

    *EUNICE comes down the steps from her flat above and enters the kitchen.
    There is another burst from the poker table.*

STANLEY: Drew to an inside straight and made it, by God.

PABLO: *Maldita sea tu suerto!*

STANLEY: Put it in English, greaseball.

PABLO: I am cursing your goddam luck.

STANLEY [*prodigiously elated*]: You know what luck is? Luck is believing you're lucky. Take at Salerno. I believed I was lucky. I figured that 4 out of 5 would not come through but I would . . . and I did. I put that down as a rule. To hold front position in this rat-race you've got to believe you are lucky.

MITCH: You . . . you . . . you. . . . Brag . . . brag . . . bull . . . bull.

STELLA goes into the bedroom and starts folding a dress.

STANLEY: What's the matter with him?

EUNICE [*walking past the table*]: I always did say that men are callous things with no feelings, but this does beat anything. Making pigs of yourselves. [*She comes through the portières into the bedroom.*]

STANLEY: What's the matter with her?

STELLA: How is my baby?

EUNICE: Sleeping like a little angel. Brought you some grapes. [*She puts them on a stool and lowers her voice.*] Blanche?

STELLA: Bathing.

EUNICE: How is she?

STELLA: She wouldn't eat anything but asked for a drink.

EUNICE: What did you tell her?

STELLA: I—just told her that—we'd made arrangements for her to rest in the country. She's got it mixed in her mind with Shep Huntleigh.

BLANCHE opens the bathroom door slightly.

BLANCHE: Stella.

STELLA: Yes, Blanche?

BLANCHE: If anyone calls while I'm bathing take the number and tell them I'll call right back.

STELLA: Yes.

BLANCHE: That cool yellow silk—the bouclé. See if it's crushed. If it's not too crushed I'll wear it and on the lapel that silver and turquoise pin in the shape of a seahorse. You will find them in the heart-shaped box I keep my accessories in. And Stella . . . Try and locate a bunch of artificial violets in that box, too, to pin with the seahorse on the lapel of the jacket.

She closes the door. STELLA turns to EUNICE.

STELLA: I don't know if I did the right thing.

EUNICE: What else could you do?

STELLA: I couldn't believe her story and go on living with Stanley.

EUNICE: Don't ever believe it. Life has got to go on. No matter what happens, you've got to keep on going.

The bathroom door opens a little.

BLANCHE [*looking out*]: Is the coast clear?

STELLA: Yes, Blanche. [*To* EUNICE.] Tell her how well she's looking.

BLANCHE: Please close the curtains before I come out.

STELLA: They're closed.

STANLEY: —How many for you

PABLO: Two.—

STEVE: —Three.

> BLANCHE *appears in the amber light of the door. She has a tragic radiance in her red satin robe following the sculptural lines of her body. The "Varsouviana" rises audibly as* BLANCHE *enters the bedroom.*

BLANCHE [*with faintly hysterical vivacity*]: I have just washed my hair.

STELLA: Did you?

BLANCHE: I'm not sure I got the soap out.

EUNICE: Such fine hair!

BLANCHE [*accepting the compliment*]: It's a problem. Didn't I get a call?

STELLA: Who from, Blanche?

BLANCHE: Shep Huntleigh . . .

STELLA: Why, not yet, honey!

BLANCHE: How strange! I——

> *At the sound of* BLANCHE's *voice* MITCH's *arm supporting his cards has sagged and his gaze is dissolved into space.* STANLEY *slaps him on the shoulder.*

STANLEY: Hey, Mitch, come to!

> *The sound of this new voice shocks* BLANCHE. *She makes a shocked gesture, forming his name with her lips.* STELLA *nods and looks quickly away.* BLANCHE *stands quite still for some moments—the silverbacked mirror in her hand and a look of sorrowful perplexity as though all human experience shows on her face.* BLANCHE *finally speaks with sudden hysteria.*

BLANCHE: What's going on here?

She turns from STELLA *to* EUNICE *and back to* STELLA. *Her rising voice penetrates the concentration of the game.* MITCH *ducks his head lower but* STANLEY *shoves back his chair as if about to rise.* STEVE *places a restraining hand on his arm.*

BLANCHE [*continuing*]: What's happened here? I want an explanation of what's happened here.

STELLA [*agonizingly*]: Hush! Hush!

EUNICE: Hush! Hush! Honey.

STELLA: Please, Blanche.

BLANCHE: Why are you looking at me like that? Is something wrong with me?

EUNICE: You look wonderful, Blanche. Don't she look wonderful?

STELLA: Yes.

EUNICE: I understand you are going on a trip.

STELLA: Yes, Blanche *is.* She's going on vacation.

EUNICE: I'm green with envy.

BLANCHE: Help me, help me get dressed!

STELLA [*handing her dress*]: Is this what you——

BLANCHE: Yes, it will do! I'm anxious to get out of here—this place is a trap!

EUNICE: What a pretty blue jacket.

STELLA: It's lilac coloured.

BLANCHE: You're both mistaken. It's Della Robbia blue. The blue of the robe in the old Madonna pictures. Are these grapes washed?

She fingers the bunch of grapes which EUNICE *has brought in.*

EUNICE: Huh?

BLANCHE: Washed, I said. Are they washed?

EUNICE: They're from the French Market.

BLANCHE: That doesn't mean they've been washed. [*The cathedral bells chime.*] Those cathedral bells—they're the only clean thing in the Quarter. Well, I'm going now. I'm ready to go.

EUNICE [*whispering*]: She's going to walk out before they get here.

STELLA: Wait, Blanche.

BLANCHE: I don't want to pass in front of those men.

EUNICE: Then wait'll the game breaks up.

STELLA: Sit down and . . .

BLANCHE *turns weakly, hesitantly about. She lets them push her into a chair.*

BLANCHE: I can smell the sea air. The rest of my time I'm going to spend on the sea. And when I die, I'm going to die on the sea. You know what I shall die of? [*She plucks a grape.*] I shall die of eating an unwashed grape one day out on the ocean. I will die —with my hand in the hand of some nice-looking ship's doctor, a very young one with a small blond moustache and a big silver watch. "Poor lady," they'll say, "the quinine did her no good. That unwashed grape has transported her soul to heaven." [*The cathedral chimes are heard.*] And I'll be buried at sea sewn up in a clean white sack and dropped overboard—at noon—in the blaze of summer—and into an ocean as blue as [*chimes again*] my first lover's eyes!

A DOCTOR and a MATRON have appeared around the corner of the building and climbed the steps to the porch. The gravity of their profession is exaggerated—the unmistakable aura of the state institution with its cynical detachment. The DOCTOR rings the doorbell. The murmur of the game is interrupted.

EUNICE [*whispering to STELLA*]: That must be them.

STELLA *presses her fist to her lips.*

BLANCHE [*rising slowly*]: What is it?
EUNICE [*affectedly casual*]: Excuse me while I see who's at the door.
STELLA: Yes.

EUNICE *goes into the kitchen.*

BLANCHE [*tensely*]: I wonder if it's for me.

A whispered colloquy takes place at the door.

EUNICE [*returning, brightly*]: Someone is calling for Blanche.
BLANCHE: It *is* for me, then! [*She looks fearfully from one to the other and then to the portières. The "Varsouviana" faintly plays.*] Is it the gentleman I was expecting from Dallas?
EUNICE: I think it is, Blanche.
BLANCHE: I'm not quite ready.
STELLA: Ask him to wait outside.
BLANCHE: I . . .

EUNICE *goes back to the portières. Drums sound very softly.*

STELLA: Everything packed?
BLANCHE: My silver toilet articles are still out.

STELLA: Ah!

EUNICE [*returning*]: They're waiting in front of the house.

BLANCHE: They! Who's "they"?

EUNICE: There's a lady with him.

BLANCHE: I cannot imagine who this "lady" could be! How is she dressed?

EUNICE: Just—just a sort of a—plain-tailored outfit.

BLANCHE: Possibly she's—— [*Her voice dies out nervously.*]

STELLA: Shall we go, Blanche?

BLANCHE: Must we go through that room?

STELLA: I will go with you.

BLANCHE: How do I look?

STELLA: Lovely.

EUNICE [*echoing*]: Lovely.

> BLANCHE *moves fearfully to the* portières. EUNICE *draws them open for her.* BLANCHE *goes into the kitchen.*

BLANCHE [*to the men*]: Please don't get up. I'm only passing through.

> *She crosses quickly to outside door.* STELLA *and* EUNICE *follow. The poker players stand awkwardly at the table—all except* MITCH, *who remains seated, looking at the table.* BLANCHE *steps out on a small porch at the side of the door. She stops short and catches her breath.*

DOCTOR: How do you do?

BLANCHE: You are not the gentleman I was expecting. [*She suddenly gasps and starts back up the steps. She stops by* STELLA, *who stands just outside the door, and speaks in a frightening whisper.*] That man isn't Shep Huntleigh.

> *The "Varsouviana" is playing distantly.*
> STELLA *stares back at* BLANCHE. EUNICE *is holding* STELLA'S *arm. There is a moment of silence—no sound but that of* STANLEY *steadily shuffling the cards.*
> BLANCHE *catches her breath again and slips back into the flat. She enters the flat with a peculiar smile, her eyes wide and brilliant. As soon as her sister goes past her,* STELLA *closes her eyes and clenches her hands.* EUNICE *throws her arms comfortingly about her. Then she starts up to her flat.* BLANCHE *stops just inside the door.* MITCH *keeps staring down at his hands on the table, but the other men look at her curiously. At last she starts around the table towards the bedroom. As*

she does, STANLEY *suddenly pushes back his chair and rises as if to block her way. The* MATRON *follows her into the flat.*

STANLEY: Did you forget something?
BLANCHE [*shrilly*]: Yes! Yes, I forgot something!

She rushes past him into the bedroom. Lurid reflections appear on the walls in odd, sinuous shapes. The "Varsouviana" is filtered into weird distortion, accompanied by the cries and noises of the jungle. BLANCHE *seizes the back of a chair as if to defend herself.*

STANLEY: Doc, you better go in.
DOCTOR [*motioning to the* MATRON]: Nurse, bring her out.

The MATRON *advances on one side.* STANLEY *on the other. Divested of all the softer properties of womanhood, the* MATRON *is a peculiarly sinister figure in her severe dress. Her voice is bold and toneless as a fire-bell.*

MATRON: Hello, Blanche.

The greeting is echoed and re-echoed by other mysterious voices behind the walls, as if reverberated through a canyon of rock.

STANLEY: She says that she forgot something.

The echo sounds in threatening whispers.

MATRON: That's all right.
STANLEY: What did you forget, Blanche?
BLANCHE: I—I——
MATRON: It don't matter. We can pick it up later.
STANLEY: Sure. We can send it along with the trunk.
BLANCHE [*retreating in panic*]: I don't know you—I don't know you. I want to be—left alone—please!
MATRON: Now, Blanche!
ECHOES [*rising and falling*]: Now, Blanche—now, Blanche—now, Blanche!
STANLEY: You left nothing here but spilt talcum and old empty perfume bottles—unless it's the paper lantern you want to take with you. You want the lantern?

He crosses to dressing-table and seizes the paper lantern, tearing it off the light bulb, and extends it towards her. She cries out as if the lantern was herself. The MATRON *steps boldly towards her. She screams and tries to break past the* MATRON. *All the men spring to their feet.* STELLA *runs out to the porch, with* EUNICE *following to comfort her, simultaneously with the confused voices of the men in the kitchen.* STELLA *rushes into* EUNICE'S *embrace on the porch.*

STELLA: Oh, my God, Eunice help me! Don't let them do that to her, don't let them hurt her! Oh, God, oh, please God, don't hurt her! What are they doing to her? What are they doing? [*She tries to break from* EUNICE'S *arms.*]

EUNICE: No, honey, no, no, honey. Stay here. Don't go back in there. Stay with me and don't look.

STELLA: What have I done to my sister? Oh, God, what have I done to my sister?

EUNICE: You done the right thing, the only thing you could do. She couldn't stay here; there wasn't no other place for her to go.

While STELLA *and* EUNICE *are speaking on the porch the voices of the men in the kitchen overlap them.*

STANLEY [*running in from the bedroom*]: Hey! Hey! Doctor! Doctor, you better go in!

DOCTOR: Too bad, too bad. I always like to avoid it.

PABLO: This is a very bad thing.

STEVE: This is no way to do it. She should've been told.

PABLO: *Madre de Dios! Cosa mala, muy, muy mala!*

MITCH *has started towards the bedroom.* STANLEY *crosses to block him.*

MITCH [*wildly*]: You! You done this, all o' your God damn inter-fering with things you——

STANLEY: Quit the blubber! [*He pushes him aside.*]

MITCH: I'll kill you! [*He lunges and strikes at* STANLEY.]

STANLEY: Hold this bone-headed cry-baby!

STEVE [*grasping* MITCH]: Stop it, Mitch.

PABLO: Yeah, yeah, take it easy!

MITCH *collapses at the table, sobbing.*
During the preceding scenes, the MATRON *catches hold of* BLANCHE'S *arm and prevents her flight.* BLANCHE *turns wildly and scratches at the* MATRON. *The heavy woman pinions her arms.* BLANCHE *cries out hoarsely and slips to her knees.*

MATRON: These fingernails have to be trimmed. [*The* DOCTOR *comes into the room and she looks at him.*] Jacket, Doctor?

DOCTOR: Not unless necessary.

He takes off his hat and now becomes personalized. The unhuman quality goes. His voice is gentle and reassuring as he crosses to BLANCHE *and crouches in front of her. As he speaks her name, her terror subsides a little. The lurid reflections fade from the walls, the inhuman cries and noises die out and her own hoarse crying is calmed.*

DOCTOR: Miss DuBois.

She turns her face to him and stares at him with desperate pleading. He smiles; then he speaks to the MATRON.

It won't be necessary.
BLANCHE [*faintly*]: Ask her to let go of me.
DOCTOR [*to the* MATRON]: Let go.

The MATRON *releases her.* BLANCHE *extends her hands towards the* DOCTOR. *He draws her up gently and supports her with his arm and leads her through the portières.*

BLANCHE [*holding tight to his arm*]: Whoever you are—I have always depended on the kindness of strangers.

The poker players stand back as BLANCHE *and the* DOCTOR *cross the kitchen to the front door. She allows him to lead her as if she were blind. As they go out on the porch,* STELLA *cries out her sister's name from where she is crouched a few steps upon the stairs.*

STELLA: Blanche! Blanche, Blanche!

BLANCHE *walks on without turning, followed by the* DOCTOR *and the* MATRON. *They go around the corner of the building.* EUNICE *descends to* STELLA *and places the child in her arms. It is wrapped in a pale blue blanket.* STELLA *accepts the child, sobbingly.* EUNICE *continues downstairs and enters the kitchen where the men except for* STANLEY, *are returning silently to their places about the table.* STANLEY *has gone out on the porch and stands at the foot of the steps looking at* STELLA.

STANLEY [*a bit uncertainly*]: Stella?

She sobs with inhuman abandon. There is something luxurious in her complete surrender to crying now that her sister is gone.

STANLEY [*voluptuously, soothingly*]: Now, honey. Now, love. Now,

now love. [*He kneels beside her and his fingers find the opening of her blouse.*] Now, now, love. Now, love. . . .

The luxurious sobbing, the sensual murmur fade away under the swelling music of the "blue piano" and the muted trumpet.

STEVE: This game is seven-card stud.

CURTAIN

Notes

(These notes are intended for use by overseas students as well as by English-born readers.)

Scene One

3   *Elysian Fields* – from 6th century BC onwards, the name given by Greek mystics to the happy resting-place for pure spirits in the Underworld.

3   *L & N tracks* – a stretch of the Louisiana and Nashville Railroad.

3   *a raffish charm* – looking attractive in a disreputable way.

3   *white frame* – a French colonial style of building: wood-frame houses in-filled with stucco or plaster, with large windows and wooden verandahs.

3   *quaintly ornamented gables* – triangular upper part of the walls at the end of the ridged roof, having attractive, old-fashioned decoration.

3   *gracefully attenuates* – softens the effect in an elegant and pleasing way.

3   *faint redolences* – hardly noticeable scents or smells.

3   *a tinny piano* – a piano which has a metallic tone, probably in need of tuning, often found in bar-rooms where jazz is played.

3   *infatuated fluency* – the flowing skill of someone who loves playing.

3   *'blue piano'* – sad and rhythmic music of Negro origin, played on a piano.

3   *Red hot! Red hots!* – hot and spicy frankfurter sausages.

3   *clip joint* – a place of entertainment, probably rather run-down or seedy, where one is likely to be overcharged or cheated.

3   *got a date* – have an arrangement to meet someone, usually someone of the opposite sex.

3   *a Blue Moon cocktail* – a drink made up of various ingredients, based on cheap whisky.

3   *you won't go out on your own feet* – you'll have to be carried out.

4   *bowling jacket* – a jacket to be worn when playing at a bowling-alley (a game in which one rolls a large ball down a track to knock over a number of wooden pegs).

4   *even money . . . odds* – the language of betting: to 'have odds' is

to have a chance of winning more than twice what one has staked. 'Even money' means having the chance of simply doubling one's stake.

4   *holler* — shout.

4   *Bowling* — (see above).

4   *a poor boy's sandwich* — a sandwich made from thick slices of bread around slices of mutton with pickles.

4   *a valise* — a small suitcase.

5   *incongruous to this setting* — looks out of place, does not belong.

5   *the garden district* — the more wealthy and fashionable part of New Orleans, near the university.

5   *uncertain manner* — hesitant behaviour.

5   *a streetcar named Desire* — a streetcar, or tramcar, running along tracks in the street. This streetcar passed up the main street of the French Quarter of New Orleans near Tennessee Williams's apartment. Its destination board read simply: Desire.

5   *Cemeteries* — another streetcar running through the French Quarter on the way to the cemeteries.

5   *six blocks* — a block is the distance between one street-intersection and the next.

5   *Elysian Fields* — (see note to p. 3).

5   *That's the party* — that is the person.

5   *She's got the downstairs . . . up* — Stella lives in the ground floor apartment and Eunice lives on the floor above.

5   *bowling alley* — (see note to p. 4).

5   *I'll go tell her you come* — a dialect corruption of 'I'll go and tell her you have come'.

5   *You welcome* — you are welcome (dialect).

5   *make yourself at home* — treat the place as if it were your home, make yourself comfortable.

6   *sort of messed up right now* — rather untidy at this moment (colloquial).

6   *real sweet* — really attractive.

6   *Uh-huh* — a sound meaning 'yes'.

6   *Por nada* — it was no trouble, don't mention it.

6   *you taught school* — you were a school-teacher (colloquial).

6   *Mississippi* — one of the Southern states of the U.S.A., part of the South's Confederacy during the Civil War (1861-65).

6   *the plantation* — a large estate on which, in the South, cotton was grown, traditionally owned by relatively wealthy families of European extraction and worked by Negro slaves.

6   *Belle Reve* — the Dubois family was of French Huguenot origins.

The name means 'Beautiful Dream'.

6 *awful hard to keep up* — take a great deal of money and effort to maintain and keep in good condition (colloquial).

6 *about to drop* — nearly collapsing with weariness.

6 *honey* — a casual term of goodwill or friendliness.

6 *set down* — sit down (dialect).

6 *I'll make myself scarce* — I will leave, go away.

6 *drop by* — go to.

6 *an' hustle her up* — and make her hurry up (dialect).

6 *closet* — cupboard.

7 *a half tumber* — a large glass that is half-full.

7 *keep hold of myself* — remain in command of my emotions.

7 *feverish vivacity* — excited, restless, uncomfortable liveliness.

7 *spasmodic embrace* — an affectionate gesture, here done in a jerky manner as if on impulse.

7 *over-light* — a light hanging down from the ceiling.

7 *merciless glare* — a harsh, fierce light that does not flatter in any way.

7 *complies* — does as asked.

7 *a convenient location* — a place near shops and transport, therefore making life easier. The phrase is often used by people trying to sell the property.

7 *liquor* — alcoholic drink.

7 *on the place* — 'on' is usually used when 'the place' is a farm or estate, whereas 'in' is more usual when 'the place' is a room or apartment.

7 *I spy* — I see something. It is the phrase or jingle used to introduce a child's game: 'I spy with my little eye'.

7 *to mix with* — a non-alcoholic drink mixed with spirits like whisky.

7 *Look'n see* — look to see if there is something there (colloquial).

7 *not with my nerves* — means that she is too upset, excited, nervous.

8 *to chase it* — to drink *after* rather than with the alcoholic drink itself.

8 *all shaken up* — feeling very upset or disturbed.

8 *Only Poe* — only the poet and story-teller Edgar Allan Poe, no-one else. Poe (1809-49) is best known for his tales of the supernatural and his dreamlike poetry.

8 *ghoul-haunted* — haunted by spirits that preyed on the flesh of corpses.

8 *woodland of Weir* — a phrase from Poe's poem 'Ulalumé'.

8 *L & N tracks* — (see note to p. 3).

8   *write me* — write to me (colloquial).

8   *The subject is closed!* — nothing more is to be said about the matter.

8   *volunteer that information* — speak of something without having to be asked.

8   *been fired* — been dismissed from her position as a teacher.

8   *nerves broke* — her state of mind and health were suddenly so badly upset that she could not continue her way of life.

8   *tamping* — pressing the end of her cigarette down into the ashtray.

8   *high school superintendent* — the man in charge of the running of a school for teenage pupils.

8   *leave of absence* — a period away from work, not part of one's usual holiday.

9   *the wire* — the telegram.

9   *one's my limit* — I never take more than one drink.

9   *look just fine* — look both healthy and attractive.

9   *watch around the hips a little* — be careful not to put on weight, not to get fatter round the hips.

9   *a feather bob* — hair cut short, in layers, to create an effect of lightness.

9   *a cherub in choir* — a childlike angel seen singing amongst a group of angels.

9   *tiny nip* — a small drink.

9   *to put the stopper on* — to be the last one, to complete the occasion.

9   *looks are slipping* — losing her good looks.

9   *haven't slipped one particle* — have not deteriorated in the slightest way.

10   *that gives much* — that bends or sinks under one's weight.

10   *be decent* — not cause embarrassment but be respectable.

10   *highbrow* — intelligent and well educated, interested in culture.

10   *Polacks* — Americans of Polish descent (slang).

10   *a mixed lot* — a group containing many different types.

10   *Heterogeneous* — made up of different elements.

10   *types is right* — it is appropriate to refer to them as 'types' rather than as people. This suggests that they are disconcertingly like stereotypes or caricatures — Stella's tone is dismissive or mocking.

10   *put up at* — stay at.

10   *get along fine* — find each other agreeable.

11   *blinded by all the brass* — so impressed by his officer's uniform that I could not recognise his faults.

11   *civilian background* — the neighbourhood and social class he belonged to before going into the army.

11   *take it* — respond to the news.

11   *on the road* — travelling as a salesman.

11   *can hardly stand it* — find it very difficult to endure.

11   *go wild* — become restless and disturbed.

11   *on his lap* — either 'with my head on his knees' or 'sitting on his knee'.

11   *an uneasy rush* — very quickly and in a troubled way.

11   *bound to* — will most certainly.

11   *take into consideration* — make allowances for, be more tolerant on account of.

11   *looked out for yourself* — acted in your own interests, with little thought for others.

11   *hold it together* — prevent it from deteriorating beyond repair or having to be sold off.

12   *'blue piano'* — (see note to p. 3).

12   *you're a fine one* — you have no right to.

12   *parade* — a formal march of people in a line, in a ritualistic or showy manner.

12   *So big with it* — the body swollen by disease.

12   *what gorgeous boxes* — how magnificent the coffins are.

12   *the Grim Reaper* — Death, traditionally represented as a hooded figure holding the long-handled blade once used to cut corn.

12   *put up his tent on our doorstep* — seemed to have decided to stay at Belle Reve.

12   *a cent of insurance* — any money to be paid at their death as a return for money paid regularly to an insurance company during the person's life.

13   *in bed with* — this has a specifically sexual meaning, 'making love to'.

13   *a cop* — a policeman (slang).

13   *is Mass out yet* — the joke depends upon 'Mass' being said with such a drawl that it sounds like 'my arse'.

13   *looks her over* — inspects her.

13   *a hoarse bellow* — a rough, husky roar of laughter.

13   *playing poker* — having a session of the gambling card-game.

13   *Yeah* — yes (slang).

13   *Break it up* — stop making so much noise in a group, go home.

13   *we was playing* — corruption of 'we were playing' (colloquial).

13   *Jax* — from Jacksonville.

13 *screen door* — a door with see-through panels, perhaps wire-mesh.

13 *implicit in* — the idea expressed by the very form of something, without having to be put into words.

13 *Branching out from* — leading off in various directions from a centre point.

13 *auxiliary channels* — secondary interests or ways of living.

14 *emblem* — symbol, representative image, crest or trademark.

14 *gaudy seed-bearer* — showy in a rather crude way, the male animal who has the power to impregnate females.

14 *sizes up* — assesses their worth, registers their good points.

14 *sexual classifications* — in his mind arranging them into groups according to how sexually attractive or not they are.

14 *determining the way* — being the element which influences how something is done.

14 *the little woman* — a patronising way of referring to his wife (colloquial).

14 *coming in town* — coming into town (colloquial).

14 *Laurel* — a town in Mississippi.

14 *not in my territory* — not within the area that Stanley travels round as a salesman.

14 *Have a shot?* — would you like a measure of whisky?

14 *I rarely touch it* — I very seldom drink it. Stanley's reply refers to the way people who *claim* seldom to drink alcohol nonetheless are often found drunk.

14 *my motto* — the set of words that sums up his way of life.

14 *when you been exercising* — a corruption of 'when you have been exercising'.

14 *How long you here for* — again Stanley drops a verb: 'how long are you here for'. It is characteristic of his style of speech.

14 *shack up* — move in, stay for a while (colloquial).

14 *wears me out* — exhausts me.

15 *take it easy* — relax, do things without strain.

15 *fallen in* — Stella has been so long in the bathroom Stanley suggests that she may have fallen into the lavatory. Blanche finds such humour difficult to take.

Scene Two

15 *completing her toilette* — putting the finishing touches to her make-up and doing her hair.

15 *blue piano* — (see note to p. 3).

15   *monkey doings* — silly behaviour.

15   *lordly composure* — accepting her kisses calmly, as if they were no more than he, as her lord and master, expected.

15   *Galatoires'* — a small but popular restaurant in the French Quarter.

15   *not going to no Galatoires'* — not going to Galatoires' or anywhere like it. The double negative is a feature of many dialect or spoken forms of the language.

15   *a cold plate* — a plate with an assortment of cold food on it.

15   *dandy* — fine, delightful (used ironically).

15   *breaks up* — ends and everybody goes home.

15   *take it* — react to it.

16   *in a hot tub* — in a bath of hot water.

16   *quiet her nerves* — make herself feel calmer.

16   *gloss things over* — describe the situation as being better than it is.

16   *that's the deal* — that is the situation. 'Deal' can refer either to a business arrangement, or to the distribution of cards in a game.

16   *have a gander* — have a look at (colloquial).

16   *bill of sale* — the document relating to the sale of the property.

16   *It seems like* — it seems as if (colloquial).

16   *give away* — given away (colloquial).

17   *Napoleonic Code* — a legal system introduced by Napoleon III of France which laid down the principle that a husband acquired joint ownership of all his wife possessed on his marriage to her. Louisiana was formerly owned by France.

17   *head is swimming* — she is unable to think clearly.

17   *swindled* — cheated.

17   *go to pieces* — lose her self-control, become upset.

17   *stalks into* — walks angrily.

17   *Open your eyes to this stuff* — look clearly at these things and understand what they represent in terms of cost.

17   *preen herself* — show off her finery, like a bird grooming its feathers.

17   *solid-gold dress* — a dress made of gold thread, as expensive as if made of unalloyed gold. Stanley is exaggerating for effect.

18   *daybed* — a bed which can be used as a divan or couch during the day.

18   *costume jewellery* — jewellery made out of paste or semi-precious stones, of no great value.

18   *safe-cracker* — a criminal who specialises in opening safes.

18   *kidding* — joking (colloquial).

18   *have different notions* — consider different things important, behave differently.

18   *You're damn tootin'* — you are absolutely right (colloquial).

19   *buttons in back* — buttons on the back of her dress, which she cannot reach.

19   *drag on your cig* — take your cigarette and inhale (colloquial).

19   *Me an' Stella* — colloquial corruption of 'Stella and I'.

19   *raided some stylish shops* — like a pirate, took goods from shops dealing in fashionable and expensive goods.

19   *a tribute* — a gift to show affection or admiration.

19   *fishing for* — making remarks in the hope of getting a compliment in reply.

20   *a doll* — a pretty young woman (colloquial).

20   *shut her up like a clam* — silenced her, made her keep her mouth shut.

20   *are took in* — are deceived by (colloquial).

20   *Hollywood glamour stuff* — the emphasis on good looks and fashionable clothes encouraged by the film industry in Hollywood.

20   *Lay her cards on the table* — be absolutely straightforward, make it clear exactly what she has to offer.

20   *wishy-washy* — vague, indefinite, insipid.

20   *re-bop* — this comes from 'be-bop', an intricate form of jazz, therefore Stanley is dismissing Blanche's chatter as being irrelevant, mere display.

20   *through dressing* — finished getting dressed.

20   *drug-store* — a shop selling medicines but also cosmetics, drinks and sweets.

20   *lemon-coke* — a coca-cola and lemonade drink.

20   *double-talk* — talk that appears to have meaning, but conceals the speaker's real intentions.

21   *vice versa* — the same idea, but in reverse.

21   *atomizer* — a perfume spray.

21   *play so dumb* — pretend to be stupid or naive (colloquial).

21   *pull that stuff* — behave in an insincere way (colloquial).

22   *made loans on the place* — lent money, with the property as a security. This kind of loan is called a mortgage.

22   *epic fornications* — sexual immorality on a grand scale.

22   *I hereby endow you* — legal language, such as used in wills, to mean that one hands on property to someone else.

23   *study these out* — examine these carefully.

23   *sheepish* — embarrassed, ashamed.

23   *blue piano* — (see note to p. 3).

23   *thrashed it out* — sorted out a problem by discussing it frankly.
23   *tamale vendor* — seller of spicy Mexican food. Tamale is seasoned meat and cornmeal baked in corn husks.
23   *Red hots* — (see note to p. 4).
24   *The blind are leading the blind* — a traditional saying.
24   *hot trumpet* — passionate, exciting music played on a trumpet, fast tempo jazz with a heavy beat.

Scene Three

24   *The Poker Night* — this was the title of an earlier version of this play.
24   *Van Gogh* — a Dutch Post-Impressionist painter with a distinctively energetic use of brush-strokes and colour (1853-90).
24   *portières* — curtains hung over a doorway.
24   *wild* — having its value decided by the players.
24   *one-eyed jacks* — the knaves of spades and hearts in a pack of cards, which, unlike the knaves of diamonds and clubs, are seen in half-profile.
24   *a shot* — a drink of whisky with nothing added.
24   *chop suey* — a popular adaptation of a Chinese food.
24   *chips* — betting money (sometimes replaced by tokens of some sort).
24   *Ante up* — raise the sum of money originally staked as a bet.
24   *Openers* — opening bids.
24   *on your high horse* — behaving in an arrogant manner.
25   *out again* — throwing in his hand, unable to continue to play.
25   *I gotta* — I have a (colloquial).
25   *Spade flush* — high-scoring hand, made up entirely of spades.
25   *a sugar-tit* — a baby's teat flavoured with sugar or syrup.
25   *lay off* — leave me alone, stop it (colloquial).
25   *Seven card stud* — a type of poker game.
25   *ole nigger* — old Negro (insulting slang).
25   *th'owing* — throwing (Steve's style of speech is indicated).
25   *lickety split* — at great speed (colloquial).
25   *puts on the brakes* — stops running.
25   *gits that hongry* — becomes so hungry (that he loses the sexual urge).
25   *frazzled* — exhausted, weary-looking.
25   *till I powder* — until I put powder on my face, improve my appearance.
25   *done in* — tired out, exhausted.

26   *to quit* — to stop playing (colloquial).

26   *kibitz* — watch a player from behind while offering advice.

26   *portières* — (see note to p. 24).

26   *call it quits* — decide this is a fair moment to stop (colloquial).

27   *a wolf* — a man whose main interest in women is merely sexual.

27   *the plant* — the factory.

27   *to get anywhere* — to win promotion, achieve some success.

27   *portières* — (see note to p. 24).

27   *a drive he has* — his force of personality.

27   *beefy* — heavily built.

27   *hens* — a dismissive expression for women, referring to them as silly, noisy domestic creatures.

27   *cut out that conversation* — stop talking.

27   *hush up* — be quiet (colloquial).

28   *Awright* — all right. (It is characteristic of Stanley to drawl and slur his words.)

28   *you in* — are you joining in this game?

28   *Xavier Cugat* — an American band leader.

28   *them drapes* — those curtains.

28   *or quit* — (see note to p. 26).

28   *get ants* — a shortened version of the saying 'Get ants in your pants', meaning to become very edgy or restless.

28   *the 'head'* — the lavatory (colloquial).

28   *pants* — trousers.

28   *spitballs* — wads of paper chewed into small balls or pellets.

28   *quarters* — 25-cent coins.

28   *piggy bank* — a china, hollow pig with a slot in the back, in which children may keep their savings.

28   *The Little Boys' Room* — a rather coy name for the lavatory.

29   *cigs* — cigarettes (colloquial).

29   *wrapper* — dressing-gown or house-coat.

29   *Mrs Browning* — Elizabeth Barrett Browning (1806-61), a poet in her own right, married to the poet Robert Browning.

29   *My tongue . . thick* — She is a little drunk, therefore cannot speak clearly.

30   *French Huguenots* — Protestants fleeing religious persecution in France from 1685 onwards who settled in the U.S.A., especially in the South.

30   *Bourbon* — an important street in the French Quarter of New Orleans, full of striptease houses and bars where jazz was played.

30   *very run down* — not in good health, tired.

30   *an old maid* – a dismissive term to describe a woman who is not married and never likely to be so, someone dull and old-fashioned.

30   *Grade school or high school* – the American system of education is divided into broad levels: grade school is an intermediate level; high school is the final stage, possibly leading to college or university education.

31   *bobby-soxers* – adolescent girls wearing the contemporary fashion for ankle socks.

31   *drug-store* – (see note to p. 20).

31   *Romeos* – young men in love. An ironic reference to Shakespeare's tragic young lover in *Romeo and Juliet*.

31   *Hawthorne* – Nathaniel Hawthorne (1804-64), one of a distinguished New England group of writers, best known for short stories such as *The Scarlet Letter*.

31   *Whitman* – Walt Whitman (1819-82), an American poet, best known for a collection of poems called *Leaves of Grass*.

31   *Poe* – (see note to p. 8).

31   *Wien, Wien, nur du allein* – a Viennese waltz.

31   *portières* – (see note to p. 24).

31   *spark of decency* – one small, possibly short-lived wish to act with humanity and courtesy.

32   *blew your top* – lost your self-control in a fit of bad temper (colloquial).

32   *sons of bitches* – general term of abuse.

33   *slow and blue* – (see note to 'blue piano', p. 3).

33   *polka dot* – a material patterned with small dots.

33   *drawers* – underpants.

33   *baby doll* – term of endearment, drawn from the lyrics of popular love songs of this period.

33   *blue piano* – (see note to p. 3).

33   *Quit that howling* – stop crying out like that.

33   *ain't comin'* – is not coming (colloquial).

33   *stinker . . . whelp of a Polack* – general insults, referring to his Polish extraction.

33   *haul you in* – take you into police custody.

34   *Potomac* – a river marking the southern boundary of Maryland, disputed by Virginia until 1671. The army of the Potomac was created to guard Washington D.C. after the Union defeat by the Confederate army at Bull Run in 1861.

34   *crazy about* – very much in love with.

34   *Naw* – no (colloquial).

34   *Set down* — sit down.

Scene Four

35   *narcotized tranquillity* — the calmness of someone who has taken
a narcotic drug.

35   *the car greased* — to have thick oil put on the car's axles.

36   *a powder-keg* — an explosive situation, easily bursting into violence.

36   *matter of fact* — unemotional, unsurprised.

36   *your fix* — your unfortunate situation.

37   *movies and bridge* — going to films and playing a card game called
bridge (also a game involving winning stakes).

37   *wore his pin* — wore the young man's ornamental pin, as a token
that they were pledged to each other in some sense — a harking back to
the chivalric tradition when a knight wore his lady's 'favour', perhaps
a scarf.

37   *ran into him* — met him by chance.

37   *Miami* — a holiday resort on the Florida coast of the U.S.A.

37   *a block long* — (see note to p. 5).

38   *throws away at the races* — casually loses by making foolish bets
at a race-course.

38   *Western Union* — one of the major telephone companies in the
U.S.A.

38   *Kleenex* — a well known brand of paper tissues.

38   *measly* — wretched, unimpresive.

38   *coin of the realm* — coins of the country's currency, rather than
notes.

39   *smooth things over* — make amends for the previous trouble, to
ease relationships.

39   *a little pocket-money* — money set aside for personal pleasures
rather than necessities.

39   *take to the streets* — become a prostitute.

39   *a bromo* — an abbreviation for a compound of bromine used to
calm the nerves.

39   *go to bed with him* — this has a specifically sexual sense.

40   *rattle-trap* — expression coined to describe the noise and rickety
state of the streetcar.

40   *bangs through the Quarter* — 'bangs' not only describes the noise
of the real streetcar, but has a sexual meaning which Blanche uses in
linking the streetcar called Desire with that sexual desire Stella feels
for Stanley.

40   *he's common* — vulgar, lacking refinement and culture or good breeding.

40   *seersucker pants* — trousers made of thin, puckered material, probably striped.

41   *swilling* — drinking greedily, like pigs.

41   *hulking* — hanging about the place with little sense of purpose (American slang). The word also suggests the bulkiness and lack of grace she associates with Stanley and his kind.

41   *Hiyuh* — colloquial greeting.

41   *darn* — corruption of 'damned'.

41   *don't know their can from third base* — don't know what they're doing. 'Can' has several slang meanings: a toilet; someone's backside; a car especially adapted to get greater acceleration; a storage battery. 'Third base' is baseball terminology.

41   *'blue piano'* — (see note to p. 3).

Scene Five

42   *on the wing* — moving about from one place to another.

42   *Forewarned is forearmed* — a traditional saying, meaning that if one has advance notice of an event, one may take steps to prevent or to deal with it.

42   *the Gulf* — the Gulf of Mexico.

42   *ain't pulling the wool over my eyes* — are not deceiving me (colloquial).

42   *staying down . . . going up* — Eunice wishes that her husband would stay down in the bar, merely drinking, but she believes that he goes upstairs to the rooms of the prostitutes.

42   *the vice squad* — a department of the police responsible for exposing and preventing prostitution, drug abuse and sex crimes or such other corruption as the law forbids.

43   *daemonic* — as if possessed by an evil spirit, frenzied.

43   *bowling shirt* — (see note to p. 4).

43   *registers* — reacts to.

43   *That hunk* — a slut (colloquial), also an insulting reference to his wife's size and aggressiveness.

43   *picked up* — collected without cost.

43   *count on* — be sure of.

43   *banging around in the army* — (see note to p. 40, 'bangs').

44   *under the impression* — is convinced (the phrase suggests that this may be an unjustified belief).

44 *I figure* — I think (colloquial).

44 *some other party* — someone else.

44 *I'm nearly out* — my supply is nearly finished.

44 *portières* — (see note to p. 24).

44 *cooing* — murmuring affectionately and indistinctly.

45 *don't I rate* — don't I deserve, am I not worth.

45 *slip through my fingers* — escape from my control.

45 *awf'ly* — awfully, very.

45 *turn the trick* — succeed in making people offer her 'protection', be attractive.

45 *I'm fading* — my good looks are going, I'm getting old.

45 *soft drink* — non-alcoholic drink, such as lemonade or coke.

46 *a shot* — a measure of whisky.

46 *hang around* — stay where one is not wanted and where one has no business.

46 *hanky* — handkerchief (colloquial).

46 *Blot* — use absorbent material to soak up liquid.

46 *a grateful drink* — she is grateful for the drink (an example of transferred epithet, the adjective attached to other than the obvious noun).

46 *our relations* — our relationship. She might with equal justification be concerned about their relations, the members of their families, in view of Mitch's mother.

46-7 *hasn't gotten a thing* — has had no physical intimacy with Blanche.

47 *'put out'* — try to make her charms obvious, sell herself.

47 *a drink under his belt* — having been drinking.

47 *bawling* — shouting.

47 *cackling* — laughing like a witch.

47 *portières* — (see note to p. 24).

47 *collecting for* — collecting money for.

47 *on the job* — while working.

47 *a dime* — a ten-cent coin.

47 *give me a light* — light my cigarette.

47 *Fifteen of seven* — a quarter to seven, 18.45 hours.

47 *blue piano* — (see note to p. 3).

48 *drug-store* — (see note to p. 20).

48 *a soda* — soda water with flavouring.

48 *Uhhuh* — a sound meaning 'yes'.

48 *make my mouth water* — make me wish I could have the same.
The language is deliberately being used in a sexually provocative way by Blanche.

48   *bashful kid* — a shy child (colloquial).

48   *Rosenkavalier* — the hero of a romantic opera by Richard Strauss.

Scene Six

49   *neurasthenic personality* — suffering from a nervous disability, likely to be perpetually under strain emotionally.

50   *Lake Pontchartrain* — a lake and park with a fairground, to the north of New Orleans.

50   *Mae West* — an American film star, well known for her buxom figure, her huskily suggestive voice and her flair for witty repartee full of sexual innuendo.

50   *shooting-galleries* — where anyone may try their skill at shooting a number of moving targets to win some prize of little value.

50   *hot tamale man* — (see note to p. 23).

50   *hangs on till the end* — stays out on the streets until the day appears really to have ended and all likely customers have gone home.

50   *Bourbon* — (see note to p. 30).

50   *owl-car* — an all-night streetcar.

50   *rise to the occasion* — behave with the vitality and wit called for.

50   *ten points for trying* — credit for effort, as a schoolchild might be given.

50   *no dice* — nothing works, one gets nowhere (gambling terminology).

50   *fingers . . . all thumbs* — her hands are clumsy.

50   *rooting in* — fumbling about inside, searching.

51   *outstayed my welcome* — remained so long that I am no longer wanted here.

51   *Eureka!* — success! The cry supposedly uttered by Archimedes when he discovered the principle of water displacement while in his bath.

51   *Pleiades* — a constellation of stars, also known as the 'Seven Sisters'.

51   *little bridge party* — a session out playing bridge. Blanche refers to them as if they were suburban middle-class women.

51   *she'll be lost* — her hopes of a secure future and respectability will vanish.

51   *get lost immediately* — lose their virtue or honour or innocence on their first evening with a man.

51   *a night-cap* — a late-night drink.

52   *joie de vivre* — happiness, pleasure in living.

52   *Bohemian* — unconventional, uninhibited in a way associated with artists who feel free of society's restrictions.

52 *Je suis . . . Armand* — I am the Lady of the Camellias. You are Armand. This refers to the romantic tragedy by Dumas fils (1848) telling of a courtesan brought back to virtue by love only to die of tuberculosis in her lover's arms.

52 *Voulez-vous . . . dommage* — Would you like to go to bed with me this evening? Don't you understand? What a pity.

52 *a damned good thing* — 'damned' is used for emphasis. Blanche realises that it would be a mistake to let Mitch recognise her sexual desires.

52 *two shots without any dividends* — two measures of whisky with nothing extra.

52 *alpaca* — wool from a long-haired llama.

52 *wash-coat* — jacket of light, washable material.

53 *work-out* — go through a routine of physical exercise.

53 *soft in the belly* — with flabby stomach muscles.

53 *in the vicinity of* — approximately.

53 *Samson* — a character from the Old Testament, renowned for his strength until weakened by the treachery of a woman he adored, Delilah.

53 *affectation of demureness* — a false display of modesty and respectability.

53 *unhand me, sir* — take your hands off me. The phrase Blanche uses is deliberately old-fashioned, referring to out-moded ideas of correct behaviour.

54 *out of bounds* — beyond what is allowed. The phrase comes from school or military idiom.

54 *old maid* — (see note to p. 30).

54 *rolls her eyes* — an expression indicating self-mockery or disbelief.

54 *Loew's State* — a cinema.

54 *Two-forty-first* — in the army, the Two-forty-first Engineers. (c.f. p. 62).

54 *putting it mildly* — understating the case.

55 *portières* — (see note to p. 24).

55 *to put up with* — to endure, manage to live with.

56 *passes on* — dies.

56 *in the quicksands* — struggling to survive. 'Quicksands' are treacherous ground where one may sink down further and further until one disappears, and struggling to escape merely worsens the situation.

57 *vacantly* — without expression, as if incapable of thought.

Scene Seven

58   *portières* — (see note to p. 24).

58   *I reckon so* — yes, I think so (colloquial).

58   *100 on the nose* — exactly 100 degrees Fahrenheit (colloquial).

58   *got th' dope on* — know the truth about (colloquial).

58   *rub her the wrong way* — behave to her in an annoying way, like rubbing a cat's fur in the wrong direction.

58   *feeding us a pack of lies* — constantly telling us lies.

58   *the cat's out of the bag* — the truth is out in the open.

59   *saccharine popular ballad* — a popular song full of sickly sentimentality, or artificial sweetness.

59   *contrapuntally* — a musical term meaning 'as an accompaniment to, but of a contrasting tempo or mood'.

59   *canary-bird* — a popular caged bird, kept for its musical song.

59   *the line she's been feeding* — the story she has been telling, the act she has been putting on (colloquial).

59   *is no lily* — is not virtuous and innocent.

59   *the plant* — the factory.

59   *'Say, it's only a paper moon . . .'* — a popular song of the late 1940s.

59   *slipped through her lily-white fingers* — (see note to p. 45).

59   *goings-on* — behaviour, disreputable happenings.

59   *Dame Blanche* — Stanley uses 'Dame' sarcastically. 'Dame' is a slang expression for a woman.

59   *turn in her room key* — give up her room, leave the hotel.

59   *Barnum and Bailey* — circus proprietors.

59   *phony* — fake, artificial (colloquial).

59   *pulled the wool over your eyes* — deceived you.

60   *honky-tonk* — a tinny, out-of-tune piano, usually in a bar-room.

60   *a penny arcade* — a place where coin-operated machines offer cheap entertainment.

60   *put on her act* — pretend to be what she was not.

60   *got wised up* — found out the truth (colloquial).

60   *same old lines* — saying the same things.

60   *same old booey* — the same absurd nonsense.

60   *loco* — *nuts* — mad, unbalanced.

60   *washed up like poison* — a failure; unable to continue; avoided by people as if she were poisonous.

60   *visiting royalty* — as if she were a member of the royal family graciously visiting the Kowalskis.

60   *Out-of-Bounds* — (see note to p. 54).

60   *No, siree, Bob!* — No, indeed (colloquial).

60   *kicked her out* — told her to leave.

60   *gotten mixed up with* — became involved with (in this case, emotionally and sexually).

61   *called on the carpet* — reprimanded.

61   *squirm* — wriggle, talk her way out of trouble.

61   *practickly* — a corruption of 'practically'.

61   *ordinance* — decree with the force of law.

61   *Possess your soul in patience* — wait patiently. A much used quotation from Shakespeare's *Hamlet*.

61   *rotten* — lacking any decency.

61   *flighty* — high-spirited and flirtatious.

62   *degenerate* — Stella means he was homosexual.

62   *pretty long time* — quite a long time.

62   *a buddy* — a friend (colloquial).

62   *the same outfit* — the same army unit.

62   *get caught* — taken advantage of, trapped.

62   *through with* — no longer prepared to have anything to do with.

62   *wised up* — in full possession of the facts (colloquial).

63   *Period* — that is an end to the discussion.

63   *P.S.* — post script, an additional thought.

63   *mapped out* — already clearly predictable, already decided.

63   *Toots* — a patronising term of endearment, here used mockingly.

63   *highball* — a drink with whisky and soda, served in a tall glass.

63   *portières* — (see note to p. 24).

63   *hectic breakdown* — the music becomes frantic and chaotic.

Scene Eight

64   *empty lot* — unoccupied or undeveloped plot of ground.

64   *drawn face* — looking strained, haggard.

64   *stood up* — deceived, kept waiting.

64   *my beau* — my man-friend, lover, admirer.

64   *cursed a blue streak* — used a whole string of obscene curses.

64   *hush . . . up* — quieten.

65   *making a pig of himself* — eating greedily and messily.

65   *Polack* — of Polish extraction (always used insultingly).

65   *A pair of queens* — members of the royal family; *or* like the queens in a pack of cards, generally of high value.

65   *Huey Long* — Huey Pierce Long (1893-1935), an American lawyer and politician, governor of Louisiana in 1928. Assassinated. Abused his powers as governor in a dictatorial manner.

66   *gonna be* — going to be (colloquial).

66   *get the coloured lights going* — have the excitement of sexual passion.

67   *taken for granted* — having one's loyalty or presence expected without further thought or persuasion, and thus undervalued.

67   *Polack* — (see note to p. 65).

67   *a shell* — used for emphasis.

67   *don't wanna* — don't want to (colloquial).

67   *false amiability* — pretended friendliness.

68   *the Greyhound* — a long-distance coach.

68   *Varsouviana* — the polka tune that haunts Blanche in connection with her husband's death.

68   *gagging* — choking and retching.

68   *Delicate piece* — a sensitive woman (colloquial). Stanley's tone is ironic and mocking.

68   *bowling shirt* — (see note to p. 4).

68   *I done nothing to no one* — I have not hurt anyone (colloquial). The double negatives are for emphasis.

68   *snapshot* — photograph.

68   *having them coloured lights going* — (see note to p. 66).

68   *showed here* — arrived here.

68   *Hoity-toity* — arrogant and condescending.

69   *El pan de mais . . . sin sal* — the words mean simply 'maize bread with no salt', from a Mexican folk-song. There is a Mexican myth which tells how God made man out of maize.

Scene Nine

69   *robe* — dressing-gown or housecoat.

70   *Y'know* — you know.

70   *uncavalier* — not the behaviour of a gentleman, unchivalrous.

70   *offers him her lips* — holds up her face to him to be kissed on the lips.

70   *a cold shoulder* — unfriendly and unresponsive behaviour.

70   *apparel* — clothes. She is using old-fashioned language as an affectation.

70   *polka* — a fast, lively dance.

70   *you dumb angel-puss* — you stupid but good-looking man (patronisingly colloquial).

70   *cross-examine the witness* — ask searching questions as a lawyer might in court.

71   *boxed out of your mind* — too drunk to think clearly.

71   *Southern Comfort* — a whisky-based drink.

71   *lapping it up* — drinking it greedily.

72   *at the plant* — at the factory.

72   *that pitch* — that story, idea put forward.

72   *malarky* — nonsense.

72   *dished out* — given to him (colloquial).

72   *you was straight* — you were honest (colloquial).

73   *put him in his place* — showed him that he was inferior to me.

73   *Rub-a-dub . . . tub* — the beginning of an old English nursery rhyme.

73   *Tarantula* — the name of a large, dangerous, tropical spider.

73   *intimacies* — sexual relationships.

73   *played out* — exhausted, unable to continue.

73   *gone up the water-spout* — disappeared suddenly, as if sucked up by a whirlwind.

74   *Flores para los muertos* — flowers for the dead.

74   *Corones para les muertos* — coronets for the dead.

74   *the paddy-wagon* — police van for taking those arrested off to jail.

75   *clean enough* — respectable enough.

75   *blue* — (see note to p. 3, 'blue piano').

Scene Ten

75   *scuffed* — scraped and marked.

75   *spectral* — ghostly.

76   *the glass cracks* — this is traditionally an omen of impending misfortune or disaster.

76   *bowling shirt* — (see note to p. 4).

76   *honky-tonk* — (see note to p. 60).

76   *a little shut-eye* — some sleep (colloquial).

76   *Yep* — yes (colloquial).

76   *fine feathers* — fancy clothes.

76   *a bolt from the blue* — a thunderbolt out of a clear blue sky, utterly unexpected.

76   *beau* — admirer.

76   *ATO* — Auxiliary Territorial Officer.

76   *relic* — something left from the past, particularly a momento of someone dead.

76   *Tiffany* — an expensive and well-known jeweller's in New York.

77   *Dallas* — a large town in Texas, a centre for the American petroleum industry.

77   *gold spouts out of the ground* — where there are profitable oil wells.

77   *sneak out of* — leave in a secretive and ashamed manner.

77   *geyser* — a forceful jet of liquid.

77   *bury the hatchet* — stop quarrelling.

77   *loving-cup* — a pledge of friendship.

77   *a red-letter night* — a memorable, significant time, with something to celebrate.

77   *You having . . . me having . . .* — Stanley uses 'having' in different ways: for Blanche the 'having' has a sexual connotation as well as meaning 'possessing'; for Stanley it means 'giving birth to', or his wife doing so.

77   *break out* — take out of its wrappings.

77   *put on the dog* — dress up specially.

78   *casting my pearls before swine* — a Biblical expression meaning wasting words of wisdom on someone incapable of appreciating them.

78   *walking papers* — orders to leave.

79   *Mardi Gras outfit* — a carnival costume of the sort worn at Mardi Gras celebrations on the day before the beginning of Lent, the Christian period of self-denial.

79   *rag-picker* — collector and seller of rags and old clothes.

79   *been on to you* — seen through your pretence.

79   *pull any wool . . . eyes* — treat this man like a fool, deceive him.

79   *Egypt . . . Queen of the Nile* — as if she were Cleopatra.

79   *jiggles the hook* — tries to alert the operator by moving the telephone receiver-rest up and down.

79   *rolled a drunkard* — robbed a drunk while he was asleep.

80   *rooting* — searching about in.

80   *Western Union* — an American telephone company.

80   *left th' phone off th' hook* — did not replace the telephone receiver properly.

80   *blue piano* — (see note to p. 3).

80   *interfere with* — make sexual advances.

81   *putting on* — what new act are you trying?

81   *rough-house* — physical violence, fighting.

81   *this date* — generally a romantic meeting arranged between a man and a woman.

81   *hot trumpet* (see note to p. 24).

Scene Eleven

81   *portières* — (see note to p. 24).

82   *Drew to an inside straight and made it* — by taking calculated chances collected a winning hand in the poker game.

82   *Maldita sea tu suerto* — curses on your luck.

82   *Salerno* — during the Second World War British and American forces landed on the Salerno beaches in Italy. Fierce fighting followed. The American Fifth Army captured Salerno.

82   *rat-race* — competition to survive and succeed in life.

82   *Brag . . . bull* — to brag is to boast, also the name of a card game. 'Bull' is a colloquial term for exaggeration or an incredible story.

82   *Making pigs of yourselves* — eating greedily and without refinement.

83   *the coast is clear* — the way clear of people, safe for her to come out.

83   *come to* — wake up, pay attention.

84   *green with envy* — extremely envious.

84   *the game breaks up* — the card game finishes.

85   *quinine* — medicine made from cinchona bark, used to reduce fever.

85   *silver toilet articles* — silver-backed mirror, comb, etc.

87   *filtered into weird distortion* — the music of the polka is introduced gradually, made strange and discordant by the accompanying jungle noises.

87   *Doc* — abbreviation for 'Doctor'.

87   *fire-bell* — an electric bell used to alert people to the danger of fire, the sound would therefore be disquieting and ominous.

87   *reverberated through a canyon of rock* — given echoes as it bounced off the rocky sides of a narrow valley.

88   *Madre de Dios! . . . mala* — Mother of God! This is a bad, bad business.

88   *Quit the blubber* — stop wailing like a child (colloquial).

88   *bone-headed* — stupid, brainless (colloquial).

88   *cry-baby* — someone who is childishly quick to burst into tears (colloquial).

88   *take it easy* — relax, calm down.

88   *Jacket* — a strait-jacket, used to restrain the violently insane.

89   *personalized* — recognisable as a human being, an individual.

89   *portières* — (see note to p. 24).

89   *luxurious* — pleasurably self-indulgent.

89   *voluptuously* — sensuously and in a manner suggestive of sexual pleasure.

90   *blue piano* — (see note to p. 3).

90   *muted trumpet* — a trumpet played with a pad placed across the horn to muffle and soften the sound.

90   *seven-card stud* — a poker game in which the bets are placed after the dealing of seven successive rounds of cards, face up.

Marlon Brando as Stanley

Vivien Leigh as Blanche

Mitch (Karl Malden) and Blanche

Blanche and Stanley

Stanley and Blanche

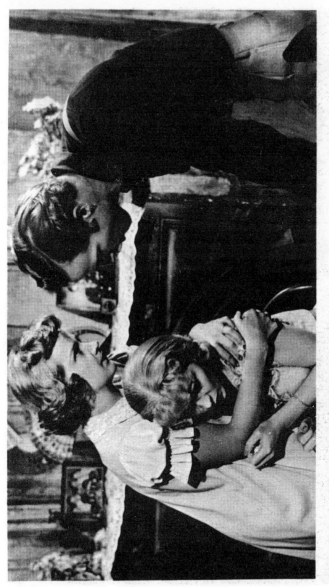

Stella (Kim Hunter), Blanche and Stanley

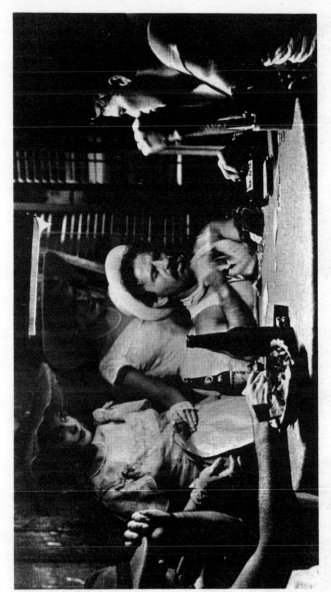

The Poker Night

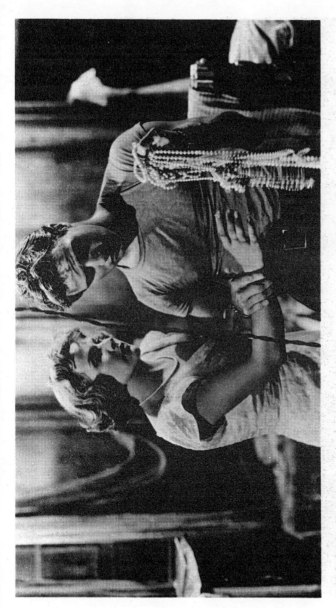

Stella and Stanley

The Matron and Blanche

The Doctor leads Blanche away

Blanche and Mitch

Stanley, Blanche and Stella

The Quarter

Questions for further study

1. To what extent is Blanche the controlling force in the play?
2. Compare and contrast the attitudes of Blanche and Stella to the story of their past selves at Belle Reve.
3. How far do the audience agree with Blanche's assessment of Stanley as an 'ape'?
4. Discuss the dramatic devices which Williams uses in the play to suggest that Blanche is doomed.
5. Stanley ripping away the paper lantern represents his destruction of lies, deceit and fantasy. Explore aspects of truth and fantasy in the play.
6. 'A play must concentrate the events of a lifetime into the short span of a three-act play. Of necessity these events must be more violent than in life' (Tennessee Williams). Examine the creation of tension as it is developed through the eleven scenes of the play.
7. In his directorial notes on the play Elia Kazan suggests that through watching the decline of Blanche '[the audience] begin to realise that they are sitting in at the death of something extraordinary [. . .] and then they feel the tragedy'. Discuss the fall of Blanche in the play.
8. Explore Williams's use of colour as it impacts upon the changing atmosphere of the play.
9. The 'visual projection of Blanche's inner life' is a key aspect of Williams's dramatic technique. How is it used?
10. The 'infusion' of lyricism in the atmosphere of Elysian Fields is created using a range of visual and aural devices. Examine Williams's creation of environment within the play.
11. 'If Blanche belongs to the crumbling grandeur of the Southern plantations, Stanley is a new American, an immigrant man of the city.' How does the play express the conflict between traditional values and the new world?

12. 'The blind are leading the blind' (Blanche, Scene II). Examine the twinned themes of sight and blindness as they are expressed through character and dramatic incidents.

13. 'Don't hang back with the brutes' (Blanche, Scene IV). Discuss the development of the character of Stanley as it is revealed, both through his own words and actions, and the perceptions of others.

14. 'The relationship between Stanley and Stella is based on his need for domination and her need for protection.' Discuss.

15. The relationship between Blanche and Mitch offers an interesting perspective on the nature of gender relations in the play. Focusing on clear examples of at least two of the relationships, explore the issues which arise.

16. 'He acts like an animal, has an animal's habits' (Blanche, Scene IV). Explore the conflicts between gentility and animal brutality in the play.

17. 'I lived in a house where dying old women remembered their dead men [. . .] Death . . . [. . .] the opposite is desire' (Blanche, Scene IX). Examine Williams's use of this theme to affect the audience.

18. The lurid reflections which fall across the walls in the final scene are a potential manifestation of Blanche's terrors and fears. Discuss the dramatic devices used by Williams in the final scene.

19. 'The language of the play is shaped by two needs: character-identification and thematic development.' Explore this statement.

20. Stella's apparent betrayal of Blanche offers the audience a clear insight into her character. Discuss the complexities of the relationship between the sisters in the light of Stella's final act.

21. *A Streetcar Named Desire* appears to be a hybrid drama: naturalistic, symbolic and poetic. Do you agree?

22. Blanche's response to the figure of the doctor in the final scene of the play is characteristic of her deep-rooted perception of the role of men in her life. Explore the range of Blanche's attitudes towards the men in the play.

23. 'To hold front position in this rat-race you've got to believe you are lucky' (Stanley, Scene XI). To what extent does Williams emphasise the role of luck in dictating the course of the lives of his characters?

24. Is *A Streetcar Named Desire* a moral play?

Methuen Drama Student Editions

Jean Anouilh *Antigone* • John Arden *Serjeant Musgrave's Dance*
Alan Ayckbourn *Confusions* • Aphra Behn *The Rover*
Edward Bond *Lear* • Bertolt Brecht *The Caucasian Chalk Circle*
Life of Galileo • *Mother Courage and her Children*
The Resistible Rise of Arturo Ui • *The Threepenny Opera*
Anton Chekhov *The Cherry Orchard* • *The Seagull* • *Three Sisters*
Uncle Vanya • Caryl Churchill *Serious Money* • *Top Girls*
Shelagh Delaney *A Taste of Honey* • Euripides *Elektra* • *Medea*
Dario Fo *Accidental Death of an Anarchist* • Michael Frayn *Copenhagen*
John Galsworthy *Strife* • Nikolai Gogol *The Government Inspector*
Robert Holman *Across Oka* • Henrik Ibsen *A Doll's House* • *Ghosts*
Hedda Gabler • Charlotte Keatley *My Mother Said I Never Should*
Bernard Kops *Dreams of Anne Frank* • Federico García Lorca
Blood Wedding • *Doña Rosita the Spinster* (bilingual edition) •*The House*
of Bernarda Alba • (bilingual edition) • *Yerma* (bilingual edition) • David
Mamet *Glengarry Glen Ross* • *Oleanna* • Patrick Marber *Closer* • John
Marston *The Malcontent* • Joe Orton *Loot* • Luigi Pirandello *Six*
Characters in Search of an Author • Mark Ravenhill *Shopping and*
F***ing • Willy Russell *Blood Brothers* • *Educating Rita* • Sophocles
Antigone • *Oedipus the King* • Wole Soyinka *Death and the King's*
Horseman • August Strindberg *Miss Julie* • J. M. Synge *The Playboy*
of the Western World • Theatre Workshop *Oh What a Lovely War*
Timberlake Wertenbaker *Our Country's Good* • Arnold Wesker *The*
Merchant • Oscar Wilde *The Importance of Being Earnest* • Tennessee
Williams *A Streetcar Named Desire* • *The Glass Menagerie*

Methuen Drama Modern Plays

include work by

Edward Albee
Jean Anouilh
John Arden
Margaretta D'Arcy
Peter Barnes
Sebastian Barry
Brendan Behan
Dermot Bolger
Edward Bond
Bertolt Brecht
Howard Brenton
Anthony Burgess
Simon Burke
Jim Cartwright
Caryl Churchill
Complicite
Noël Coward
Lucinda Coxon
Sarah Daniels
Nick Darke
Nick Dear
Shelagh Delaney
David Edgar
David Eldridge
Dario Fo
Michael Frayn
John Godber
Paul Godfrey
David Greig
John Guare
Peter Handke
David Harrower
Jonathan Harvey
Iain Heggie
Declan Hughes
Terry Johnson
Sarah Kane
Charlotte Keatley
Barrie Keeffe

Howard Korder
Robert Lepage
Doug Lucie
Martin McDonagh
John McGrath
Terrence McNally
David Mamet
Patrick Marber
Arthur Miller
Mtwa, Ngema & Simon
Tom Murphy
Phyllis Nagy
Peter Nichols
Sean O'Brien
Joseph O'Connor
Joe Orton
Louise Page
Joe Penhall
Luigi Pirandello
Stephen Poliakoff
Franca Rame
Mark Ravenhill
Philip Ridley
Reginald Rose
Willy Russell
Jean-Paul Sartre
Sam Shepard
Wole Soyinka
Simon Stephens
Shelagh Stephenson
Peter Straughan
C. P. Taylor
Theatre Workshop
Sue Townsend
Judy Upton
Timberlake Wertenbaker
Roy Williams
Snoo Wilson
Victoria Wood

Methuen Drama Contemporary Dramatists

include

John Arden (two volumes)
Arden & D'Arcy
Peter Barnes (three volumes)
Sebastian Barry
Dermot Bolger
Edward Bond (eight volumes)
Howard Brenton
  (two volumes)
Richard Cameron
Jim Cartwright
Caryl Churchill (two volumes)
Sarah Daniels (two volumes)
Nick Darke
David Edgar (three volumes)
David Eldridge
Ben Elton
Dario Fo (two volumes)
Michael Frayn (three volumes)
John Godber (three volumes)
Paul Godfrey
David Greig
John Guare
Lee Hall (two volumes)
Peter Handke
Jonathan Harvey
  (two volumes)
Declan Hughes
Terry Johnson (three volumes)
Sarah Kane
Barrie Keefe
Bernard-Marie Koltès
  (two volumes)
Franz Xaver Kroetz
David Lan
Bryony Lavery
Deborah Levy
Doug Lucie

David Mamet (four volumes)
Martin McDonagh
Duncan McLean
Anthony Minghella
  (two volumes)
Tom Murphy (five volumes)
Phyllis Nagy
Anthony Neilson
Philip Osment
Gary Owen
Louise Page
Stewart Parker (two volumes)
Joe Penhall
Stephen Poliakoff
  (three volumes)
David Rabe
Mark Ravenhill
Christina Reid
Philip Ridley
Willy Russell
Eric-Emmanuel Schmitt
Ntozake Shange
Sam Shepard (two volumes)
Wole Soyinka (two volumes)
Simon Stephens
Shelagh Stephenson
David Storey (three volumes)
Sue Townsend
Judy Upton
Michel Vinaver
  (two volumes)
Arnold Wesker (two volumes)
Michael Wilcox
Roy Williams (two volumes)
Snoo Wilson (two volumes)
David Wood (two volumes)
Victoria Wood

Methuen Drama World Classics

include

Jean Anouilh (two volumes)
Brendan Behan
Aphra Behn
Bertolt Brecht (eight volumes)
Büchner
Bulgakov
Calderón
Čapek
Anton Chekhov
Noël Coward (eight volumes)
Feydeau
Eduardo De Filippo
Max Frisch
John Galsworthy
Gogol
Gorky (two volumes)
Harley Granville Barker
  (two volumes)
Victor Hugo
Henrik Ibsen (six volumes)
Jarry

Lorca (three volumes)
Marivaux
Mustapha Matura
David Mercer (two volumes)
Arthur Miller (five volumes)
Molière
Musset
Peter Nichols (two volumes)
Joe Orton
A. W. Pinero
Luigi Pirandello
Terence Rattigan
  (two volumes)
W. Somerset Maugham
  (two volumes)
August Strindberg
  (three volumes)
J. M. Synge
Ramón del Valle-Inclán
Frank Wedekind
Oscar Wilde

For a complete catalogue of Methuen Drama titles
write to:

Methuen Drama
A & C Black Publishers Ltd
36 Soho Square
London W1D 3QY

or you can visit our website at:

www.acblack.com